F.I.R.E Starter

Financial Independence Retire Early

5 Steps You Need to Take to Retire a Millionaire

Gene Reid

Table of Contents

Thank You & Dedication

This book is dedicated to . . .

    My sisters who have supported me through my trials and tribulations. To my niece who has been the biggest joy of my life. This book is also a dedication to my auntie who has known me the longest and makes me feel like I am capable of anything. To my best friend who has been there since the 5th grade. To a new friend that told me I have a lot of information to share with the world. To my soon to be wife who took me to Aruba so I could slow down and finally put this together.

Introduction—So You Want to Get Rich

The Secrets They Didn't Teach You In School

Take note, people! You have been fed a ton of nonsense about retiring. You're supposed to work until you're 65, but that's bull pucky! What if I told you that you could retire early and be financially independent. The time has come for you to take charge of your financial future and tell corporate America to f--- off!

Let's start by discussing the ways in which schools have misled you. They advise us to work for a respectable company and retire at age 65. But that's a bunch of nonsense! You can become financially independent and enjoy a debt-free life. Folks, I'm not just blathering fairy stories here.

I'm here to share with you the principles of the F.I.R.E. movement and how you can become financially free. We'll talk about everything, including using IRAs and 401(k)s and getting out of debt. Additionally, you'll discover how to set up a budget, save money, and steer clear of debt.

Also, don't forget to have fun! You can still have fun even while you're trying to save money. Come on, you only have one life to live! (Hashtag YOLO, am I right?)

So come along with me on this financial independence adventure. You'll know more about your financial condition by the end of this book, and you'll be well on your way to retiring early. Who knows, perhaps you'll spend your golden years in Disneyland. Just don't hold it against me if, after spending too much time with Mickey and friends, you start to think you're a real-life princess. Seriously, just kidding.

Chapter 1: Taking Inventory

You must understand your spending before starting on your path to financial independence and early retirement. This phase can be uncomfortable, but as they say, no pain, no gain! Seriously, setting up a budget and cutting personal expenses are crucial. Tracking your monthly expenses and estimating your net income are good places to start. Sort your spending into categories to see where you can cut costs, pay debt and save. Focus on a three to five year debt repayment plan and establish an emergency fund that is 12-18 months of expenses. As you pay off debt you can save money first for your emergency fund then for significant midterm goals like a wedding, vacation, or a home purchase. Long-term objectives can last for many years and include retirement planning and college savings for your kids.

Creating Your Budget That Won't Break Your Bank Account

You must actively work on your budget each month; it is not something you do once. You'll frequently need to change your expenditures to live within your means. Variable expenses, like eating out, should be the first thing you reduce when attempting to change your budget. If possible, limit your monthly outings to one or two rather than three or four a month, a week a day – you get what I mean. Keep in mind that even the smallest savings can add up if you stay the course. Get laser beam focused on your budget and where you spend your hard earned cash. This fixation with keeping track of your spending is essential to knowing if you are on track. It's also important to reevaluate and alter your budget when life changes occur like a pay raise or more money is now available since you paid off your debt.

Overall, keep in mind that building a portfolio to achieve financial independence and early retirement is a marathon, not a sprint. Be persistent in achieving your objectives, use patience, and, most importantly, enjoy yourself. You deserve it!

Building the Perfect Budget

First and foremost, you need to keep a close eye on your spending. My friend, I'm talking eagle eyes. Reduce all of your wasteful spending, including that streaming service you hardly ever use and that expensive cup of coffee. Do you really need a rainbow cocoa-infused frappe every day, I mean, really? No, I do not believe you do. I'll share a quick secret recipe with you: Blend espresso or black coffee with milk and sweetener; then, add ice to a to-go mug and top it off with whipped cream, caramel, and chocolate syrup. Instant savings of $89 a month! That is a significant amount that could be used to pay off debt or to use to save and invest.

When it comes to investing, I recommend paying off your debt first, especially if the interest rate is high. But don't worry, you can still accumulate that nest egg for an early retirement. Although it might entail working a little harder than most of your friends who intend to work until they are 65, I assure you that it will be worthwhile in the long run.

Creating a budget can seem a little intimidating at first, but don't let that deter you. As soon as you accomplish your short and long-term goals, treat yourself to a movie or a nice dinner. Just be careful not to overdo it or I will judge you. Just kidding. Keep a record of your income and expenses and change your budget as necessary. My friend, you've got this!

Different Types of Budgets and How to Pick The Best One For You

Hello, fellow friend who likes having money! Are you sick and tired of constantly feeling poor? Do you intend to leave the workforce before you turn 65 years old? Then pay attention because I'm about to explain the beauty of budgeting.

Let's start by being clear that budgets are not a form of punishment. They're not some terrible diet that makes you subsist on tap water and ramen noodles. Budgets, however, serve as your wallet's personal trainer. They assist you in living a life you want and deserve.

Consider this: Would you just wing it and hope for the best or would you have a strategy, a timetable, and a target in mind? Obviously a strategy! Budgeting is similar to that, except it is for your financial life. If you want to prevail in the financial marathon, you must have a strategy, a timetable, and a target.

Don't worry, budgeting doesn't require you to be an expert in arithmetic. In actuality, it's quite easy. Simply keep track of your earnings and outlays, identify where your money is going, and develop a strategy to save more and spend less. See? Easy.

But budgets are boring, I know some of you are saying. They suck all the pleasure out of life! Let me tell you something, though: that is a lot of nonsense. Actually, creating a budget can be fun, especially if you have the correct tools. It is fun because you can see progress in the efforts and fun because you are accomplishing your financial freedom goals.

There are several personal financial apps available that make creating a budget simple. Personal Capital, Mint, and You Need A Budget (or YNAB, as the cool people call it) are a few of my favorites. You may categorize your spending using these applications, track your income and expenses, and even establish financial objectives like debt repayment or retirement. A few of them are also entirely free! Who doesn't enjoy free things? As I always say, free is better than cheap.

So get started with budgeting right now if you're prepared to take charge of your money and stop living paycheck to paycheck. Your future self will be grateful. Who knows, though? You might even find that you have a secret aptitude for spreadsheets. Hey, stranger things have happened.

Budgeting Methods

Now you know a few of my favorite tools.

Let us talk about the different budget methods.

Everyone's different, and before you start going down the road of financial independence and retire early, you must pick the best budgeting strategy for you. The proper budgeting method can vary depending on your income, goals, spending habits, and even your lifestyle, so there's no one-size-fits-all budget. Once you have a clearer idea of what tool is right for you, you can start choosing the method.

Pay-Yourself-First Budget

Take note, take note!

I've got a great tip for all of you rebels against tracking every single dollar you spend. The "Pay Yourself First" budget method is for you.

Here's how it works: as soon as you get money you put a percentage away, say 10%, for your savings and investing accounts. Having first saved and invested you can now concentrate on paying your bills and paying down debt.

Of course, not everyone should use this approach. Before you go headfirst into "Pay Yourself First," you should at the very least have a general notion of what your monthly expenses are. However, it's still much more manageable than attempting to keep track of every dollar you spend.

Give the "Pay Yourself First" strategy a try if you're seeking a means to begin accumulating wealth without driving yourself crazy with a budget. I know your future self will appreciate it.

Envelope System Budget

Budgeting can be intimidating, so do not be alarmed. With the help of budgeting apps like Good Budget, you may modernize the traditional envelope approach of managing your finances.

The envelope system is a traditional budget method. You use actual envelopes and label them with the names of your current expenses like rent, utilities and groceries. When the money in an envelope is gone, it's gone. The following pay period is when you can resume spending in that area.

Thankfully, you no longer need to maintain boxes of envelopes scattered across your home. Most bank apps now have an "envelope" option that allows you to divide your money across various "envelopes" that are intended for different expenses. Once all of your money is allocated to your various envelopes you will be able to determine how much money you have for saving and investing. Do not be discouraged if in the beginning you have very little money for saving and investing. The goal is to get rid of your debt so you can concentrate on saving and investing.

50/30/20 Budget

I have to admit that the 50/30/20 budgeting approach is a contemporary budgeting method. It is often called the

Needs/Wants/Savings budgeting method. Your income is divided into three using this strategy. You set aside 50% of your salary for needs like rent, food, and utility costs. You set aside 30% of your salary for luxuries like vacations and TV subscriptions, delivery meals, and the occasional bubble tea. Finally, you set aside 20% of your salary for debt reduction, investments, and savings.

This approach is a fantastic way to begin budgeting without worrying about every dollar you spend. Like going on a date with the understanding that the tab will be divided 50/50. No more awkwardly debating whether to order the lobster or how much to tip.

It is okay if you need to modify your percentages because you have a large amount of debt. Reduce your spending so you can put more money toward paying down your debt. Keep in mind that you are in charge of your spending. What percentage goes towards Needs/Wants/Savings is up to you. Just decide what the percentage is and move forward with your F.I.R.E. plan.

The 'No' Budget

Simply put, this budgeting approach advises you to limit your expenditures and avoid using your nonexistent funds. Basically, do not spend money that is not currently in your bank account. You must monitor your bank balance, like a hawk, or use a budgeting tool. You must be aware of your monthly expenses and when they are due. You must, also, treat your savings and investing goal as an expense and put those monies away on a predetermined day every month. Whatever is left, spend on a nice dinner out.

Sounds easy enough, doesn't it? Prepare for a fight because telling yourself "no" can be harder than a piece of beef jerky. However, there isn't a single, effective approach to budgeting. What works for your friend may not work for you.

Just pick a budgeting method so you can get closer to being debt free and saving and investing for retirement.

Expense Slayer: Conquering Your Financial Overhead

Bravo! You are tracking your expenses with a spreadsheet or budgeting program. The next step is to keep track of your spending and begin cutting back. If your spending exceeds your income, you may need to do some significant cost cutting. The first cost cutting measure would be to concentrate on paying off your debt and refrain from accruing additional debt.

You need to prioritize your expenses if you're spending more than you're making. Rent, utilities, food expenses, and paying off any debt should be at the top of your priority list. After doing all of that, if you're still in the red, it could be time to consider strategies to raise your income or further reduce your costs.

Tips on Reducing Expenses

By now, you have done your monthly budget and your financial assessment. Now it's time to start tracking your spending habits.

One of the first things you can do is to reevaluate your subscriptions. Many people have monthly subscriptions for streaming TV services, phones, or the internet. Ask yourself, "how much do I use it?" or "can I live without it?" Then, when you unsubscribe from a service, make sure you also unsubscribe from any newsletters that may entice you to return. You want to cut all ties because advertisers are like magnets: they have a great way of drawing you in and enticing you to buy.

Decreasing Your Utility Bills

Utility bill reductions might be a great method to increase your financial savings. Naturally, you don't have to shiver in a cold home or sit in a pitch black room. However, it might be possible to reduce your electricity costs without compromising your comfort. Typically, 12% of your household budget goes toward paying utilities costs. Therefore, it's crucial to pay attention to how much electricity and gas you use. Wash your clothes only when there is a full load or try air drying your clothing on a line. Additionally, you can lower your electricity costs by turning off your TV when you're not watching it. Keep your home heating and cooling on only when you are home or on a timer. Additionally, your local government may offer tax incentives to assist in switching to a more energy-efficient heating and cooling system. In this way, you can save a small sum on taxes while also helping the environment.

Reducing Your House Expenses

Now, if you're like the majority of people, your rent or mortgage payment is a fixed expense that takes up a large portion of your income. However, that does not exclude you from finding ways to save and invest. If your home has a spare room, you may rent it out and earn some additional money. Alternatively, you could consider short-term rentals like Airbnb or Peerspace. If you rent an apartment, you might be able to negotiate a rent decrease in exchange for making certain repairs with your landlord or sign a lease for longer than a year to get a decrease in rent or a rent concession

Additionally, if you own a home, think about refinancing your mortgage to benefit from reduced interest rates and lower monthly payments.

Consolidate Your Debt and Crush Minimum Payments

If you have credit cards, you may be aware of how damaging revolving credit can be. Credit cards, i.e. revolving credit, can be such a heavy burden because you do not have a defined pay off date. Here is how it works: If you have a balance of $15,000 on a credit card aka revolving debt and your annual percentage rate (APR) is 16% you divide 16% by 365 days (16%/365). This will tell you how much interest is accruing daily. To use our example 16% divided by 365 equals 0.0004 (16%/365=0.000438356164384). To determine how much interest you owe at month's end multiply what you owe by the accrued interest by the number of days in the month. For example sake, let us say you owe $15,000 in the month of July you would multiply 15,000 by 0.0004 by 31 the monthly interest charges would be $203.83 (15,000.00 X 0.000438356164384 X 31=203.83). You can avoid interest payments that cause your balance to grow, if you pay your balance off at the end of the month. If you are unable to pay off the full amount then interest will accrue on the remaining balance.

To get out of the minimum monthly payment club and avoid revolving credit you may want to consider a debt consolidation loan. With a debt consolidation loan you have a fixed installment loan. Installment loans provide you with a fixed number of payments and provide you a payoff date. A debt consolidation loan enables you to consolidate all of your payments into a single, manageable monthly payment and may even result in a lower interest rate. This can be a fantastic option to receive a set fixed monthly payment and a lower interest rate. But you might find it difficult to obtain it if you have a low credit score.

Another option for debt consolidation is a debt management plan, with a consumer credit counseling agency. You can minimize your interest rates and payments by taking advantage of the services provided by these nonprofit agencies. They negotiate lower payments for you with credit card providers and provide advice on how to settle your debt. So check out Consumer Credit Counseling of Buffalo and Money Management International if you're looking to get out of debt and lower your credit card interest rates.

Whatever you do, try and avoid the companies that tell you not to pay your bills for months or even years. Their goal is to position you so you can negotiate paying a lower overall total balance. I get what they are trying to do but that puts you in place where you are reported to the credit bureaus as delinquent with your payments. Thus putting you in a position where your credit remains bad and it prolongs your inability to save and invest for an early retirement. Also, if they are able to successfully negotiate a settlement for an amount lower than your original debt, your creditor may be required to file a 1099-C for with the IRS. This means you could be responsible for paying the remaining balance that you did not pay your creditor to good ol' Uncle Sam.

Adjust Your Insurances

Let's discuss auto and home insurance. Insurance can be expensive. Review your policies annually to confirm if you are getting the best rates and coverage. Do your research and look around for businesses that offer reduced premiums. Joining associations like AAA, no, not the batteries, might also result in lower auto insurance premiums. Consider switching from a full coverage policy to a liability policy if your car is paid off and or increase your insurance deductible to reduce your premiums. When you increase your deductible you are letting the insurance company know that you are willing to pay a certain amount towards the repair of your car, if you have an accident, prior to the insurance company's contributions towards the repair.

When it comes to potentially lowering your home owners premiums consider making your home safer by installing alarm systems, smoke detectors or upgrading your electrical and heating systems. These improvements could position you for reduced premiums. So, in order to save a ton of money, do yourself a favor and turn your house into a fortress or at the very least, a place with a reliable alarm system.

Seriously, whether it is your car or your home I suggest making a call to your insurance company to see how you can reduce your premiums.

Eating at Home

Your wallet may thank you for pre-planning your meals! Finding the time to cook each day can be challenging, but with a little planning, you can significantly reduce your food expenses. Prepare meals on the weekends and this will allow you to have individual servings for the rest of the week. Meal prep allows you to avoid the effort of cooking every day and it allows you to avoid paying for lunch while at work or doing take out for dinner. Having something delicious and healthy to eat daily is also a bonus.

And remember to bring a list with you when you go grocery shopping. It can help you avoid making unnecessary purchases and keep you on track with your food plan. Don't forget to look into any loyalty reward programs and coupons your supermarket may provide. Loyalty reward programs and coupons can provide excellent savings on the things you frequently buy. So make a list, schedule your meals, and start saving money!

Using Only Cash

Hey there, do you want to hear an insane idea?

Change all transactions to cash only! Although it may sound like something from the Stone Age, trust me—it actually works! Consider this: you set up automatic debit payments for all of your bills and then withdraw the remaining funds in cash. This will make it simple for you to keep track of your spending and prevent overspending. Additionally, paying with cash will make you feel like a baller.

What Is Your F.I.R.E Number

Retirement planning can be quite difficult and daunting, but there is a tactic known as The Rule of 25 that can be of assistance in planning for retirement. It has nothing to do with feeling young forever, so don't worry, although that does sound nice. You can calculate The Rule of 25 by taking the amount of money you expect to spend during retirement and multiplying it by 25. For example, if you expect to live off of $50,000 a year once you are retired, you multiple $50,000 x 25. The number you will need in this example is $1.25 million in your retirement account. Think about the type of lifestyle you'll lead after retirement. Spend more money after you're retired if you want to! Just keep in mind that you'll also need to save extra.

Factors to Consider With The Rule of 25

So you want to retire early and lead a stress free life, huh? Let's discuss how you can accomplish that now.

First off, you may need to disregard The Rule of 25. That's for people who wish to put off retirement till they are 65. In our 40s or 50s, we plan to retire, baby! But here's the thing: if you want to retire early, your investing approach will need to be a little more creative and possibly aggressive with your investment strategy.

The Rule of 25 often estimates your required savings amount depending on your annual expenses. However, it doesn't account for factors like inflation, market swings, or the possibility that you'll live to be 100. And let's not overlook those unforeseen costs like medical expenses. Therefore, be thoughtful to budget in advance for those kinds of costs Therefore, if you intend to retire earlier than 55, you might want to think about using the rule of 30 or 35 instead.

Oh, and if you intend to lead a lavish lifestyle in retirement, you had better start making plans right away. Having no debt and a sizable savings account are the keys to an early retirement. Additionally, if you intend to purchase that posh retirement home, make sure to begin saving for it years in advance.

There you have it. If you're ready to be a little creative with your investment approach and prepare in advance for unforeseen expenses, retiring early is absolutely feasible. Go out there right away and begin living your best life!

The 4% Rule

On to The 4% Rule now. According to this rule, you should only take out 4% of your whole portfolio each year to ensure that you have enough money to endure during your 30-year retirement. You should know that William Bengen, a financial planner, developed this formula by examining historical market and inflation data from the 1990s.

The 4% Rule states you need to multiply your retirement savings by 4%. For instance, if you have $1.25 million in savings, you can anticipate receiving $50,000 a year in retirement income. Remember that 4% is not an unbreakable rule. Depending on variables like inflation and how soon you wish to retire, you can change the percentage up or down.

You can make it the 5% or 6% rule, you can take that much money out of your whole portfolio if you believe your portfolio will perform better than the market. Just keep in mind that there are numerous things to take into account when applying these guidelines. Ultimately, you can determine the most effective retirement plan by using The Rule of 25 or The 4% rule.

Calculators

Want to become financially independent and a millionaire? You do, of course! Who wouldn't want to enjoy life without being concerned about money? You don't have to be an expert in arithmetic to make it happen, so don't worry. Calculators are here to take care of the grunt work for you!

Mortgage Calculator dot com has a super handy calculator to determine when you'll become a millionaire. You can even factor in compound interest and inflation, so you get the most accurate results possible. The millionaire calculator is a bit tricky to find, but don't fret. Just type in https://www.mortgagecalculator.org/calcs/millionaire.php and you're good to go. For our UK pals, Monevator has a similar calculator in pounds, not dollars. Check it out at https://monevator.com/millionaire-calculator.

To achieve Financial Independence Retire Early (F.I.R.E.), you must now begin saving and investing as soon as possible. Yes, you might need to make some sacrifices, but I assure you that it will be well worth it! Just keep in mind that life can be unpredictable, so don't be afraid to make adjustments when necessary to reach your objectives.

Cheers to a bright financial future!

Chapter 2: Eliminating The Debt That's Sucking Your Bank Account Dry

Today many Americans are burdened by a heavy debt load. Unfortunately, most of us did not learn about personal finance in school, and as a result, American families are on average over $100,000 in debt. Collectively, American households have 15 trillion in debt. This staggering amount of consumer debt is auto loans, credit card debts, mortgages, and personal loans.

Oftentimes, it can seem like you will never be able to dig yourself out of debt when you're simply paying the minimum. Let's face it, your bank is simply stating "we'd love to make money off of you" by having you make minimum payments. But have no worry, my friend; there are solutions to deal with your debt and get rid of the weight that debt has put on you.

Unsecured -- Revolving Debt

Unsecured debt is sometimes like dating: you have no security and no idea where it's going. Unsecured debt is not backed by collateral such as a car or house. Credit card debt is an example of unsecured revolving debt. Credit card interest rates are frequently high because there is no asset for the lender to repossess should you default.

Like I discussed earlier, there is no predetermined fixed duration or maturity date, and the balance due on a credit card is calculated daily. That's correct, the debt cycle never ends! If you don't pay your debt by the due date, the creditor will add interest to the total that is still owed.

Let us take the example below. Your $1,400 credit card amount, with a 16% interest rate, will be paid off in 45 months if you make the $42 monthly minimum payment. You will pay $468 in interest fees overall. This is presuming you don't incur any more fees during this time and pay your bills on time.

Monthly Payments	START DATE	PAYOFF DATE	TOTAL INTEREST
$42.00	December 2022	September 2026	$468

You may save money and pay off your debt considerably faster if you can afford to pay more than $42 each month. Your $1,400 credit card balance will be paid off in 38 months if you pay $48.30 per month. Overall interest will total $388. This is assuming that you don't accrue any more fees during this time and that you pay your payments on time.

MONTHLY PAYMENTS	TOTAL SAVINGS	MONTHS TO PAYOFF
$48.30	$83	37
$55	$41	32
$63	$195	27
$74	$241	23
$84	$273	19

Secured installment–Fixed Debt

On the other hand, secured debt is like a stable relationship. You know where you stand. With secured debt, the lender has collateral, like your car or house, which they can repossess if you are unable to pay. With secured debt, you have a predetermined payment schedule and a time frame to adhere to, which makes it simpler to organize your finances and know exactly when the debt will be paid off.

Paying-Off Your Debt

Identifying the type of debt you're in is the first step to getting out of it. Make a list of all of your debt, starting with the largest to the smallest. Next, sort them based on your debt or the interest rate. Once you've sorted everything out, decide on the most effective strategy for paying off those troublesome expenses.

The Best Ways to Pay Off Your Debt — Without Robbing the Bank!

Hey there, debt-crushing machine! If you missed it earlier, I provided some advice on how to use consumer credit counseling to manage your debt. But did you know that these organizations can assist you in negotiating reduced interest rates with your credit card lenders? They take these reduce interest rates and use the debt avalanche or debt snowball strategy to pay off all of your debt in as little as five years. Please note that these are techniques you can do without using a credit counseling agency. It just might be harder to negotiate lower interest rates for yourself. But hey, nothing beats a failure but a try.

Debt Snowball

Ah, the age-old conundrum of whether to use the debt avalanche or snowball approach to pay down your debt. Let's examine the differences between the two to determine which is best for you.

Regardless of interest rates, you should list your debts in order of smallest amount owed to largest amount owed. On all debts, you make the minimum payment, with the exception of the lowest, which receives all of your spare cash until it is paid off. Once that debt is paid off, you take the money that was used to pay off the first debt and add that to the minimum payment of the next smallest debt owed and resume the process. You continue this payment method until all debts are paid off.

Let's imagine, for illustration purposes, that you owe $10,000 on a car loan and $2,000 on credit cards and $15,000 personal loan. Even though the auto loan has a higher interest rate, you would prioritize paying off the credit card debt first when using the debt snowball strategy. You would then go on to the car loan once you had paid off the credit card debt and then on to the personal loan.

The main benefit of using the debt snowball strategy is the psychological lift you receive when you pay off one bill after another. You feel a sense of accomplishment from it, which inspires you to keep going. The drawback is that if you don't prioritize the debt obligations with the highest interest rates.

Debt Avalanche

Let's now discuss the debt avalanche strategy. Regardless of the balance, this strategy calls for listing your debts in order of highest interest rate to lowest interest rate. All of your debt receives the minimum payment, but for the one with the highest interest rate, which receives all of your additional funds until it is paid off. Once all debts have been paid off, go on to the debt with the next highest interest rate and repeat the process.

The main benefit of using the debt avalanche strategy is that you'll eventually pay less in interest. The drawback is that it can take longer to pay off your bills and you would not get the psychological benefit of paying off debts seeming sooner.

Which approach is best for you? Your personal preferences and financial position will determine what you do. The debt snowball strategy can be the best option if you require that psychological push to stay focused. But if long-term financial savings are more important to you, the debt avalanche approach can be a better option.

The most crucial thing to keep in mind is to start paying off your debt. The final result is the same, whether you go for the debt snowball or debt avalanche strategy: financial independence and retire early. #FIRE

In the next chapter we'll discuss how much money you need to have in the bank before you start investing. Warning: saving and investing is more involved than just finding change in your couch cushions.

Chapter 3: Emergency Fund – Why You Need One and How to Build It

Let's be clear about one thing: you need to get your finances in order before you start daydreaming about retirement! Pay off your debts first, and then start an emergency fund to save for a rainy day.

How to Build Your Emergency Fund

Let's now discuss emergency savings and how it will support your F.I.R.E plan. These funds act as your personal financial superheroes, appearing just when you need them to save the day. Your emergency fund has got you covered whether it's sudden auto repairs, unforeseen medical expenses, or a job loss.

Consider your emergency fund as your own personal safety net. The goal is to have enough money saved up so that, in the event of an emergency, you won't have to turn to credit cards, personal loans or family.

What should your savings goal be, you ask? The guideline is to have enough money set aside to pay for your household expenses for six to eight months. The more you can save, though, the better!

Now that you know how much you spend each month, you can calculate how much you ought to put in an emergency fund. This is why coming up with a budget is crucial. Although it may not seem like the most interesting thing in the world, I assure you that it is worthwhile.

The average American household spends over 60% of its income on things like housing, food and transportation, according to the U.S. Bureau of Labor Statistics Consumer Expenditure Surveys (2021). So, at least 60% of your monthly expenses should be covered by your emergency fund. But if you really want to win, have your emergency fund pay 100% of your expenses.

Suppose you have $2,000 in monthly expenses. You'll require $6,000 to have a three-month emergency reserve and $12,000 for six month reserve. Simple math, right? However, your spending plan and financial strategy will determine how much you need to save each month to achieve that objective. Do you use the 50/30/20 budget method which is 50% on needs 30% wants 20% savings or the pay yourself first approach? Take a look at your budget to see what you can set aside for an emergency fund.

Bottom line: If you want to accumulate wealth and become financially independent, having an emergency fund is essential. It functions as a kind of financial safety net that can prevent you from going under when unanticipated things happen.

Putting Your Plan Into Practice

As we focus on becoming debt free and financially independent there are sacrifices we might have to make in order to save money. You might sell your car and take public transportation for a while. You might get on a prepaid phone plan instead of the expensive postpaid plans. You may stop clothes shopping for a while. If you go out for dinner and to the movies three times a week, reduce it to once a week. All the money that you are saving should go towards your emergency fund.

The Best Places To Deposit Your Emergency Fund

You should place your emergency fund where it can grow safely. A classic savings account with easy access and high-interest rate is ideal. The logic behind this is that an emergency is usually unexpected, so having quick access to withdraw that money is essential. Placing it in a high-yield savings account is also a good idea. Do an Internet search for NerdWallet to get a listing of banks that have the best APRs. Remember to pick a bank that is FDIC insured. That means your money is protected up to $250,000. Please whatever you do if you are going to use PayPal or Venmo make sure your money will be eligible to be in one of their pass through banks. If it is not, your money will not be FDIC insured because PayPal and Venmo are not banks.

Where Does Your Savings Really Come From?

Your savings should primarily come from the income you earn on your job and from a side hustle or two. If you do not make enough to save after paying all of your bills then you need a side hustle. A side hustle can be anything, from walking dogs to selling tee shirts. Side hustles are basically freelancing jobs that you start and operate in addition to your full-time work. They're a terrific way to supplement your income. They can even grow into startups or small enterprises in some situations. This is exactly where we are going to focus on—your own company or side hustle—because this is where you are more likely to earn money and achieve your financial goals faster. The main question here is what type of side business you should choose: A service business or a product business.

Service-Based Businesses

Let me just say that a service-based business can be sweet! You don't need to think about what good you are producing, how it will be delivered to the customers, or do special fulfillments like gift-wrapping. No, you only need your knowledge and talents. Of course, you'll need to consider what you're providing and how much you'll charge, but that's nothing in comparison to the time it takes creating and developing a completely new product. Plus, you smart business person, you, are already conducting market research by determining what people want and how much they are willing to pay for it.

Product-Based Businesses

While I'm sure you are quite savvy, for the sake of clarity, it is worth mentioning that a product based business sells physical goods. Product based businesses sell tangible items. It could be you're building some fantastic coffee tables or creating the most wonderful hair pomade ever. However, once you have your product, you need to sell it aggressively while keeping a close eye on quality assurance. Customers won't just materialize on your doorstep, so you want to keep them coming back for more. Who wouldn't want some lovely, lovely word-of-mouth promotion?

Product-based businesses have the cool ability to expand, which is awesome. Even though you may begin as a one-person operation, before you realize it, you're employing others and generating income even while you're not working. It's about establishing a company and seeing where it takes you, not just about replacing your day job. And if you're fortunate, you might someday grace the cover of Forbes.

How To Kick Instant Gratification to the Curb and Master The Art of Saving

Short term, mid term and long term goals are the three buckets of money you will typically create in your journey to being finally independent. Savings goals that you can reach in a year or two are referred to as short-term goals. Mid-term savings goals often span a period of three to five years. Long term goals are five or more years in the future. It is in the long term goals that your actual F.I.R.E planning occurs.

You must establish goals for saving and investing if you want to achieve financial freedom and retire early. The first step is to group your objectives according to how long it will take you to attain them. A vacation or other short-term objective will require different amounts of time to save than, say, a down payment on a home. To monitor your progress, you should establish separate savings accounts for each of your objectives.

You could be asking, "But how many savings accounts do I need?" I understand what you're thinking. So, that depends on your objectives. You can check to determine if you are on track for each particular goal by having multiple savings accounts. Ally Bank offers you the ability to have one savings account with the ability to break into 10 buckets. This means you can set up many buckets for each savings goal you have with Ally Bank's online banking platform, naming the buckets things like "emergencies," "vacation," "home," and "education." Additionally, Ally offers "boosters" that automatically transfer funds from your primary savings account to your other saving objectives.

Like Ally Bank, CapitalOne 360 Performance allows you the ability to break your savings into buckets. You can also set up separate savings accounts for your different saving objectives. You can have as many 25 buckets with CapitalOne for your various savings objectives. One of CapitalOne's draws is the ability to visit a brick and mortar location.

Saving for Short-Term Goals

Let's face it, we all have short-term objectives, whether they be putting money down for a dream vacation or building an emergency fund. You must start saving right away if you want to accomplish these goals. The good news is that you can choose from a variety of savings account types.

For short-term objectives, traditional savings accounts and certificates of deposit (CDs) are excellent options. With conventional savings accounts, a bank statement makes it simple to keep track of your deposit amounts. While CDs feature greater interest rates, you must lock your money away for a set amount of time and there may be a penalty for early withdrawal.

Money markets accounts, while often used for midterm goal savings, are another great savings vehicle. They provide comparable interest rates but have stricter minimum balance requirements and withdrawal restrictions.

So there you have it, statement savings accounts, CDs, and money market accounts are savings vehicles you should consider using for your short term goals. So, if you do not have a savings account go out there today and get one.

Saving for Mid-Term Goals

Mid-term goals can range from school loan repayment to new automobile purchases to home renovations. Prioritize your goals and establish reasonable deadlines. You wouldn't want to lose motivation, would you? I advise setting up "digital buckets" in your savings or money market account for each mid term goal. This makes it simple for you to monitor your progress.

Saving for Long-Term Goals

Are you ready to ensure your financial freedom through investing? Of course, you are! Setting long-term goals also entails having money for your retirement. But wait, let's talk strategy before you start maxing out your retirement savings.

Prioritizing your goals is the first thing you need to do. Planning ahead is crucial because retirement might last up to 30 years. Determine your F.I.R.E number, using The Rule of 25. Remember The Rule of 25 states that you multiply your planned annual retirement income by 25. The resulting number is your F.I.R.E. number.

Now that you have your F.I.R.E. number, first begin to establish a long-term savings account with 12 to 18 months' worth of living expenses. That is of course after you save your 6-8 months emergency fund. This will shield you from selling equities during a bear market, which could jeopardize the overall health of your retirement portfolio. Again, I repeat, be sure you've established an emergency fund before you begin investing.

Once your long term account is established you can now move on to investing in retirement accounts like 401(k), 403(b), 457 or Thrift Savings Plan (TSP), as well as a Traditional IRA or Roth IRA. The 401(k), 403(b), 457 or Thrift Savings Plan (TSP) are employer offered plans and the Traditional IRA or Roth IRA are accounts individuals can open up on their own. You should maximize your contributions to these tax-advantaged retirement plans. If you can't contribute the maximum amount, no problem. Invest as much as your budget will allow, and when your financial situation improves, raise your contribution amount.

Chapter 4: How The Rich Protect Their Money with Wealth Insurance

Hello, my wise financial friend, in this chapter we will discuss how insurance is a part of your financial freedom plan.

Wealth Insurance 101

Let's begin by defining the term "wealth insurance." In essence, it's a life insurance policy that aids in maintaining your family's financial stability in the event of your death. Funeral fees, house payments, college tuition, and other living expenses that your loved ones would find it difficult to pay for without your income can all be covered with the money from a life insurance policy.

You and an insurance company enter into a contract for life insurance. Your beneficiaries will receive a lump sum payment, known as a death benefit, in return for your regular premium payments when you pass away.

You have a choice between whole life and term life insurance when considering to include life insurance in your financial plan.

Whole life vs. Term Life

As long as you continue making premium payments, whole life insurance covers you for the rest of your life. It divides your premium payments into two "envelopes." Your family receives your death benefit, which is covered by the first "envelope." The second "envelope" is a savings account known as the cash value.

A portion of your premium is invested in the cash value, which increases over time tax-deferred. You may borrow against the cash value or withdraw from it, but if you do so, your beneficiaries will receive less money if you don't repay the loan before you die.

Although the cash value growth rate varies from policy to policy, it frequently takes years for the total cash value to exceed the amount of all premium payments, and occasionally it never does. Insurance sales people will attempt to sell you on the cash value feature, but you shouldn't assume that investing in a low-return cash value account would be as profitable as investing in index funds.

Contrarily, term life insurance only provides death benefits. It offers no-cash value insurance for a predetermined term such as 5, 10, 15, 20, or 25 years. The premiums are often lower and the death benefit is bigger because there is no cash value. This means that your loved ones will get a bigger payout to help with expenditures if you pass away during the course of your policy.

Invest the Remaining

You'll probably notice a sizable price difference when comparing the pricing of a whole life policy to a term life policy. For example, a term policy for a 30 year old woman could be as little as a $15.81 monthly premium for a $100,000 death benefit and a $100,00 whole life policy for that same 30 year old woman could be as much as $300 monthly premium. If you have $300 for life insurance you could save for retirement sooner by spending $15.81 on term insurance and $284.19 to build your emergency fund and invest in your retirement. Buying term insurance and saving and investing the rest means your death benefit won't be impacted if you have to take money out.

If you already have an emergency fund set up, you may use the extra cash to increase investment in your retirement.

The main purpose of life insurance is to provide your loved ones with financial security following your passing. Life insurance is a wise decision if your spouse, significant other or children depend on you financially.

Chapter 5: Investing Techniques, The Rich Don't Want You to Know

You've heard it time and time again: you got to save for retirement. Well, how do you go about doing that? Luckily for you, you have purchased this book.

In the following pages, you will learn about the power of investing in tax-advantaged retirement savings plans, such as a 401(k), 403(b), 457(b) Plan, a Thrift Savings Plan (TSP) and Individual Retirement Accounts (IRA). You will learn about the power of compound interest and why getting started right away can be a benefit to your retirement portfolio.

In previous chapters, savings was the focus. Savings is for emergencies and life events like car repairs, medical expenses, and family vacations. You use a savings account because it is liquid and is readily available. Can you say ATM? Investing in index funds is playing the long game. Investing in index funds is what will ignite your F.I.R.E Starter plan. There is some risk but not investing is just as risky. As an example, the chart below will demonstrate the difference between placing your money in a high-yield savings account, with an average annual return of 1.75% and investing it in the S&P 500, which over the past 20 years has produced a 10% return. Now, there are a lot of numbers in this chapter, but bear with me, it's not as hard as it looks.

YEARS	HIGH YIELD SAVINGS ACCOUNT 1.75%	S&P 500 INDEX FUND 10%
YEAR 1	$10,000	$10,000
YEAR 5	$10,906	$16,105
YEAR 10	$11,894	$25,937
YEAR 15	$12,972	$41,722
YEAR 20	$14,147	$67,275
YEAR 25	$15,429	$108,347
YEAR 30	$16,828	$174,494

Take a look at the chart. If you put a one time savings amount of $10,000 in a savings account earning 1.75% interest at the end of 30 years you would have $16,828. Sounds good, right? But wait there's more. If you take that same $10,000 and invested in an S&P Index fund at 10% at the end of 30 years you would have $174,494. Now that is the making of a good retirement. The S&P 500 is one of the safest investments out there since it tracks the 500 largest companies in the U.S. The entire economy would have to collapse for you to fail. Now keep in mind past performance does not mean that the results will be the same but there is enough historical data supporting the fact that S&P should be a part of your F.I.R.E Starter plan.

You still don't believe me? Well, consider this. If you contribute $10 a day which is $3650 a year to the S&P 500, assuming it will give you a 10% annual return every year. You could potentially have $660,430 after 30 years. $10 a day is the price of an expensive cup of coffee and lunch every day. That's F.I.R.E Starter money!

YEARS	CONTRIBUTIONS	TOTAL VALUE
1 YEAR	$3,650	$4,015
5 YEARS	$18,250	$22,493
10 YEARS	$36,500	$59,502
15 YEARS	$54,750	$120,393
20 YEARS	$73,000	$220,578
25 YEARS	$91,250	$385,413
30 YEARS	$109,500	$660,430

The S&P 500 might not always give you an annual return of 10%. Some years it's more, at other times it is less, but either way, you'd be earning a lot more than just letting it sit in your bank account.

By now you are saying everyone knows the stock market is speculative. It is a gamble. I am going to take a gander and say you have played the lottery, maybe you play it every week or maybe you do not but you know someone who does. Just stick with me for a minute. The average price of a Powerball ticket is $2. Playing once a week means $8 a month is spent on the lottery. Do you know what the chances are of you winning it? Well, the odds to win one million dollars in the Powerball lottery you have to be 1 in 11,688,053.52. In the Mega Millions, your odds are 1 in 12,607,306 to win the same one million dollars. As you can see in the table above, just by adding $10 each day, you are likely to become a millionaire in 30 plus years. If you invest more into your investment account, you can retire sooner than 30 years. Essentially, any money you spend on the lottery, you would be better off adding to your investment account.

Bonds vs. Mutual Funds vs. Index Funds

Investing

Investing is similar to going on a shopping spree for things like stocks, bonds, index funds, and real estate that will make you richer over time. You have a variety of alternatives to choose from, similar to a buffet, except instead of food you are filling you plate with things such as stock to own a portion of a company or bonds to act as a lender. The purpose of investing is to outperform traditional savings methods by accelerating the growth of your money and by generating some additional income by earning dividends.

Stocks

In investing, you purchase assets like stocks, bonds, index funds, and real estate. The goal of your investments is to have them appreciate over time and generate income in the form of dividend payments or capital gains. It's similar to having a money tree, however more work is required to care for and water it.

Stocks act as miniature slices of a company that you can buy and sell. When companies want to raise capital for things like research and development they often acquire that funding by selling slices aka stocks. You can possibly earn more money from the company's future revenues the more shares you purchase, increasing your portion of the pie.

Bonds

In exchange for regular interest payments, a bondholder loans money to a company or the government for a predetermined length of time. When the bond matures, the bond's issuer pays the investor her or his money back. Since the investment will generate fixed payments for the duration of the bond, the term "fixed income" is frequently used to describe bonds.

Bond interest rates can be fixed or variable. Companies and governments issue bonds for a variety of reasons like the construction of roads, hospitals, and schools, as well as company expansion. The caveat is that there is always a potential that the borrower would stop making payments, which could result in the loss of your investment. It's crucial to do your homework so you can make informed decisions.

Mutual Funds

Mutual funds have existed since 1924. In fact, the Massachusetts Investors Trust (MITTX) was established in 1924 and still exists today. There are over 137,000 mutual funds in existence today. There is a fund for every type of investor: from those that want to focus on social responsibility to those that only invest in companies with adorable animal logos. The logo thingy, while made up by me, hopefully gives you an idea about the vast types of mutual funds that exist.

Mutual funds make investing simple. With one investment amount your money purchases shares in numerous companies. Mutual funds come in a variety of forms, such as bond funds, stock funds, emerging market funds, international funds, and index funds.

Mutual funds may be the solution if you are seeking a stress-free approach to diversify your portfolio. These funds invest your money, together with the money of other investors, in a variety of different companies. Most mutual funds have 50 to 150 companies in their portfolio. So you won't have to worry about losing all of your money like you could potentially by investing in one or two companies directly.

Bond Funds

A mutual fund that only invests in bonds is known as a bond fund. Bond funds specialize in making investments in debt securities such as corporate bonds, government treasuries, and mortgage-backed securities. For many investors, investing in bonds through a bond fund is more cost-effective than purchasing individual bonds. They are a fantastic method to provide your portfolio with a source of income through dividends earned. Bond funds, unlike individual bonds, do not have a maturity date for the repayment of principal; hence the principal invested may change occasionally. Additionally, the difficult task of deciding which individual bonds to acquire and sell is handled entirely by the fund managers.

Stock Funds

Compared to individual stock purchases, stock funds allow investors to save time and effort by investing in the common stock of publicly traded corporations. These funds, which may contain both growth and value stocks, can be separated based on market capitalization and sector. Long-term appreciation should be a stock fund's main goal. Investors can diversify their portfolios and possibly reduce risk by purchasing stock funds. But it's important to remember that stock funds can also fluctuate based on the market and the performance of particular companies. Before investing in stock funds, it's important to do your homework, think about your financial objectives, and assess your risk tolerance. Stock funds can be great for those who are active investors.

Active investors monitor their buying and selling with the goal of hoping they will beat the market.

International Funds & Global Funds

International funds invest in businesses based outside of the US, giving your portfolio the further diversification. Global Funds, invest in companies in the US and outside the US. Both international and global funds allow you to benefit from the potential growth of foreign companies. That's right, people, you can use international and global funds to unlock the economic potential of emerging and long standing economies.

Index Funds

Index funds are passive mutual funds. They are like a laid-back surfer who is simply riding the stock market's waves. They reflect the success of the market and follow particular indices, like the S&P 500. Index funds provide diversification and low operating expenses compared to other mutual funds because they do not require a high end fund manager to actively pick stocks. They have consistently outperformed actively managed mutual funds, making them a crucial component of any F.I.R.E. Starter Plan. Index funds are for passive investors, like you and me, who want to have investments that we can hold for a long time and mirror the market.

Getting Your Expectations in Order – What Returns Should You Expect?

A return is any money you gain on your investment. Returns are typically expressed in dollar amounts or any other fiat currency over a specified period but can also be described as a percentage. Over the past 20 years, the S&P 500 index funds have outperformed almost 90% of actively managed mutual funds. The S&P 500 historical average is a yearly return of almost 10%. That is compounding yearly profits in your retirement investment portfolio. Raise your hand if you are not interested in growing your money via returns in the form of dividends and growth.

Return–Who Wants Profits?

Returns, or profits, are any gains you make when revenues exceed expenses. When it comes to investing, it is any money you have made from your investments. For example, as an investor in index funds, you generally see a profit when the price of the index fund goes up and from dividends. Dividends are the profits the company is sharing with you. To get to financial independence sooner than 65, you want to select reinvest the dividends when opening your index fund. This selection will allow the dividends to be used to invest in more shares. This way, more of your return profit income will work for you.

Average Stock Market Returns

The S&P 500, average market return is close to 10%: well 9.67%, to be exact. For illustration purposes, let us round up to 10%. Remember that investing in index funds is part of your long-term financial roadmap. The table below depicts the average return of the S&P 500 through the different periods in time.

PERIOD	AVERAGE STOCK MARKET RETURN	AVERAGE STOCK MARKET RETURN ADJUSTED FOR INFLATION
5 YEARS (2017 TO 2021)	17.04%	13.64%
10 YEARS (2012 TO 2021)	14.83%	12.37%
20 YEARS (2002 TO 2021)	8.91%	6.40%
30 YEARS (1992 TO 2021)	9.89%	7.31%

Since 2000, three major events have impacted the stock market unfavorably: the dot.com bubble in 2000, the housing crisis in 2008, and the recent COVID-19 pandemic. In each case, the market came back up, as it always does. This is your retirement plan. This is your financial independence plan. In this book's savings for long-term goals section, I discussed how you should have at least 6 to 18 months saved in a savings account. You will live off of this money when the market has a downswing.

Stock Market Recovery Techniques

Investing in the stock market can at times be risky but there is a simple technique to make your investing journey less stressful: dollar cost averaging!

The term "dollar-cost averaging," or simply "DCA," refers to consistently investing in your index fund regardless of whether the market is in an up swing or a down swing. Don't worry; most discount brokerage companies will allow you to automate DCA. Suppose you put $100 into an S&P 500 index fund in January at a $5 share price. In February, you still put in $100 even when it drops to $3 a share. It drops further to $2 in March, but you remain steadfast and invest another

$100. In April and May you do not waiver and continue to invest at $100 a month with share prices at $6 and $6.50 respectively. As the below chart demonstrates, at the end of this five month investing period you will have 135 shares that value at $878. DCA allows you to take advantage of down markets. You are able to purchase more shares when the stock market is down.

MONTHS	INVESTMENT	SHARE PRICE	PURCHASED UNITS	TOTAL SHARES	TOTAL VALUE
1	$100	5	20	20	$100
2	$100	3	33	53	$159
3	$100	2	50	103	$206
4	$100	6	17	120	$720
5	$100	6.5	15	135	$878

What does this tell us? If you make the calculations, even though the share price went down and up over the months, your average purchase price is $4.50 (5+3+2+6+6.5=22.5 divided by 5). $4.50 even though in three of those months, the shares of that stock were above $4.50. However, the actual average price you have paid for your 135 shares is, in fact, lower. Since you've paid $500 for 135 shares, your average price per share is $3.70 ($500/135). As you can see, DCA spreads out the risk by allowing you to make investment purchases at regular intervals regardless of market performance. The downturns are like you investing when there are bargain basement prices.

Why Markets Always Crash – and How You Can Survive It

Okay, Okay, I know you think this is part of the book where I tell you about the Tulip Blub Crash of the 1600s in the Netherlands or give you multiple reasons why the stock market crash of 1929 happened in the U.S. Heck, I even like discussing the Dot com bubble of 2000 but would that help you in your mission to retire early.

Before we dive into the nitty-gritty, let's start with some definitions, shall we?

A bear market is when the stock market decreases by 20% or more.

In contrast, a bull market occurs when stock prices skyrocket and everyone is wealthy. Okay, so maybe not everyone, but you get the idea. When the stock market increases by 20% following a 20% loss is the official definition.

A crash occurs when the market declines by 20% or more and things truly start to go south. It resembles the evil twin of the bear market.

A correction is a decline of more than 10% but less than 20%. It is as though the market is saying, "My bad. I'll take care of that for you."

Since its founding in the 1700s, several stock market crashes have occurred. Despite crashes, the stock market always bounces back. The question often asked when the market crashes—is how long it will take to recover and grow. As an investor, you should know how to prepare for these inevitable events. You should also see this as a great sale and an opportunity to put DCA to work.

When the market crashes, you will see a sudden drop in the overall stock market, which can be attributed to various things. There is no rule for when a crash happens; it just happens, and everyone can see it. It is highly unpredictable. As I have discussed before, at the time of this writing, the COVID-19 crash of 2020 is the most recent crash.

There are a few things you can do to mitigate some of the losses that can be associated with bear markets. The first thing is to understand that predictions of crashes are never possible. Always be debt free or on a game plan to pay off debt. Anything higher than 8% is considered a high-interest debt. This has to do with the market's average annual return, which is around 8% to 10%. Usually, credit card debt and some personal loans are the ones with the highest interest rates. It would be best if you made a plan to tackle them and be able to manage them.

Secondly, having an emergency fund is crucial. Readily available money can help you when things are not going well. For example, when crashes happen, people tend to lose their jobs, so having an emergency fund that equals at least six to eighteen months of monthly expenses can come in handy.

Lastly, having a diversified portfolio that includes index funds will mitigate losses the stock market experiences. This is because different sectors will lose more than others. Not every company in the S&P 500 will experience a downturn; there is a good possibility that some companies will prosper from the downturn.

I cannot guarantee that markets will always recover because I cannot see the future. Dang, it! But history and my illustration below show that markets always bounce back: they recover.

Listen, I get it. Seeing the market drop is a nail-biting time. Seeing the market decline may even cause you to feel heart palpitations. But you now know the market, historically, has always recovered and that buying your favorite companies using DCA will allow you to buy them at bargain basement prices.

Now having purchased this book, you understand and can handle these swings in the market, which are inevitable given the nature of the market. When markets drop, it can be nerve-wracking, but selling your investments out of fear could hurt your investment F.I.R.E Starter plan and cause you to lose out on some great bargain days. You will benefit from staying the course with your investments if you wish to ride through the rough patches and reap the rewards of the upswings. The longer you hold on to an investment, the better your chances of making a profit. To give you some context, I have included a chart that shows the S&P 500's performance between 1986 and 2020, which includes the years of Black Monday in 1987, the Dot com Bubble in 2000, the Subprime mortgage crash of 2008, and the coronavirus pandemic crash of 2020, in most of the years that crashes happened, the S&P 500 still had positive returns or was able to mitigate most of the downturn.

YEAR	OVERALL MARKET CRASH (%)	S&P 500 RETURNS (%)
2020	-34%	18.4%
2008	-56%	-37%
2000	-48%	-9.10%
1990	-20%	-3.10%
1987	-34%	5.25%
1980	-27%	32.42%
1973	-48%	-14.66%

A Short History of Historical Crashes

Sigh.

I will give a short and very brief history to appease my history buffs.

As I have stated before, predicting a crash is nearly impossible. What we can do is review the annals of history to understand the main reasons behind the most important stock market crashes in history.

If you think stock market crashes have happened recently, you are mistaken. Even if the stock market as we know it is relatively recent, the economy and the financial world have existed for quite some time. The first economic crash ever recorded dates back to 1637 in the Netherlands. It was called the "tulip mania bubble," and it happened because of tulip bulbs. The government issued contracts for tulip bulbs that reached remarkably high prices, but then, as with any market bubble, they suddenly collapsed. Tulips had been introduced to the country, raising the flower's cost. This tulip mania was a socio-economic phenomenon that economists had no idea existed at the time, especially since the concept of a stock market had only been around since 1611 in the Netherlands.

Since then, there have been many other crashes of paramount significance, such as the financial crisis of 1791/92 in the U.S., the Paris Bourse crash of 1882, the Brazilian "Encilhamento" in 1890, and even the Wall Street crash of 1929, but let us focus on more recent stock market crashes.

The infamous "Black Monday Crash" of October 19, 1987, represented the biggest percentage drop in one day in the annals of the American stock market. The Dow Jones and S&P 500 both experienced greater than 20% declines. The erratic trading environment and general lack of market liquidity were to blame for this disaster. Due to the magnitude of the decline, circuit breakers were put in place, which can stop all trading for 15 minutes if the stock market falls by more than 7%. Another 15-minute break will be allowed if the drop falls below 13%. Trading stops for the day if the stock market keeps falling and reaches a 20% drop. We can draw lessons from this incident and take precautions to avoid such crashes in the future.

During the summer of 1990, Iraq made the decision to invade Kuwait, which led to a dramatic increase in the price of oil. And would you believe it? The Dow Jones experienced a decline of around 18% over the course of the subsequent three months. Ouch! This fall was the beginning of an economic contraction that lasted for an entire year and a half.

Now, let's jump ahead in time to the year 2000 where we are currently experiencing a large bubble that is commonly referred to as the dot com bubble. The dot com bubble is also referred to as the "tech bubble" or the "internet bubble." It was in the late 1990s when the NASDAQ Composite stock market index performed wild acrobatics, which caused it to soar over 400% between 1995 and March of 2000.

During that tumultuous time period, many prominent figures in the fields of technology and communication experienced devastating setbacks. Companies such as Global Crossing and Worldcom, are examples of those that filed for bankruptcy or were completely destroyed. Even enormous giants of the era, such as Cisco Systems and Amazon, were dealt significant blows to their market capitalization during this period. From 1995 until 2000, new disruptive technology hit the market, the thirst for new technology spread like wildfire; people quickly adopted tech, and before you knew it, everything went haywire. The fact that it was so simple to launch new businesses as a result of historically low interest rates was one of the primary causes of this bubble: this crash. There were a lot of eager business people who just couldn't help but dive right in and invest in tech start ups. These start ups after spending all of that money from their venture capital funding found themselves in difficult financial positions when the bubble ultimately burst. They did not see a profitable end in sight. That placed a real dent in the pockets of venture capitalist because many of these start ups failed and caused venture capitalist to loose huge wads of cash and these start up failures caused venture capitalist to reevaluate their business plans. The NASDAQ index experienced a staggering decline of almost 80 percent from its high by October 2002 rolled around. What a wild journey on the technological Ferris wheel!

Let's jump on the nostalgia train and talk about the financial crisis that occurred in 2007 and 2008. Nearly every nation on the face of the earth, from the good ol' United States of America to countries in Europe and Asia, felt the effects of that tremendous disaster. And who do you think was the star of the show?: the housing market. I repeat, the bubble that had formed in the housing market, ladies and gentlemen caused the financial crisis! It was just like a ticking time bomb that was about to go off at any moment. In order to forestall a full-scale calamity on the world's financial markets, the government of the United States was forced to step in and save a number of major financial institutions.

So that was the past, now let's jump forward in time to the most recent major event, which is the crash of the stock market in the year 2020, which features none other than the infamous COVID-19 corona virus pandemic. The events leading up to this crash followed a simple trajectory. The entire world went into lockdown, and the market responded by saying, "Gulp!" It began with "Black Monday," then continued with "Black Thursday," and finally, we were blasted with "Black Monday II." It was like a three-part series of anarchy on the stock market! However, on the bright side, the impact of this crash was temporary. By the end of 2020, the market had already started picking itself up and took its first steps toward recovery.

And now, here we are in the current day, with a Russian invasion of Ukraine, a crisis in the global supply chain, a drop in the value of bitcoin, and inflation that is out of control. It's like a never-ending amusement park filled with unpredictability out there! Who can predict how the market will react to these upcoming events? But keep in mind, my investing friends, that when it comes to investing, you should always think in the long term. Conduct research, maintain your vigilance, and use that information to guide your decision making.

Phew! That was an exciting ride on the financial history Ferris wheel. But hey, let's not forget the important lessons we can gain from all of these highs and lows. Continue to make investments, never stop learning, and don't ever forget to smell the flowers, they are attractive after all.

Rule of 72

The Rule of 72, sometimes called the "Power of Compound Interest," is a mathematical formula that allows you to estimate how many years it will take for your money to double.

Rule: To find out when you double your investment, divide 72 by the expected rate of return.

Let's have a look. If you're expecting a 9% annual compound rate, you will divide 72 by 9, and you will see that it would take you eight years to double your investment. Now, if your initial investment was $2,000, then in eight years it will be $4,000; in 16 years it will be $8,000 in 24 years it will be $16,000.

To further illustrate the power of the Rule of 72. Let us look at how long an initial investment of $3,650 doubles at 8%, 9%,

10%, 11%, and 12%, in the illustration below. With an initial investment of $3650 at 8% in 25 years you would have $24,997 at 9% you would have $31,474, at 10% you would have $39,547, 11% you would have $49,587 and at 12% you would have $62,050.

YEAR	INTEREST RATE				
	8%	9%	10%	11%	12%
0	$3650	$3650	$3650	$3650	$3650
5	$5,363	$5,616	$5,878	$6,150	$6,433
10	$7,880	$8,641	$9,467	$10,364	$11,336
15	$11,578	$13,295	$15,247	$17,464	$19,979
20	$17,012	$20,456	$24,555	$29,427	$35,209
25	$24,997	$31,474	$39,547	$49,587	$62,050

Taxable Accounts

Ah, the fascinating world of money management, where we navigate the treacherous terrain of taxable accounts and capital gains!

So, let's talk about taxable accounts, shall we? Imagine you're at a party, ready to feast on all the delicious tax benefits and tax-free retirement withdrawals. But wait! These taxable accounts are like that party pooper who forgot to bring the food and drinks. No perks, no tax benefits, nada! Your hard-earned earnings from these accounts will be taxed annually. Oh, the disappointment! Seriously though, taxable accounts are investment or savings accounts that do not offer any special tax benefits. Examples of taxable accounts include some brokerage accounts, savings accounts, money market accounts, and checking and savings accounts. Earnings from these accounts are subject to annual taxation, unlike tax-advantaged accounts such as IRAs or 401(k)s.

Alright, let's get into the nitty-gritty of checking accounts, savings, CDs, and money markets. When you make money, in the form of interest, from these accounts, it's considered regular income – just like your paycheck. No special treatment here, folks! That means they won't get any fancy tax breaks or exemptions, and their fate lies in your income tax rate. So, keep that in mind as you manage your finances and taxes!

Now, onto the mysterious realm of investment income from taxable accounts. Investment income refers to the money earned from various investments such as stocks, bonds, mutual funds, real estate, and other financial instruments. It includes the returns generated from these investments, such as dividends, interest, capital gains, and rental income. Investment income is subject to taxation, and the specific tax treatment depends on the type of investment and the holding period. Investment income is taxed as regular income. Dividends, which are the profits from your investments, have a unique feature. If you hold on to those dividends for at least 61 days within a 121-day period, a bit peculiar I know, they qualify for lower long-term capital gains tax rates.

Now, let's meet the caped crusaders of the investing world - short and long-term capital gains! Short-term gains are like those restless souls who can't wait for anything. If you buy and sell assets within a year, they're treated just like ordinary income by the taxman. Nothing fancy here, folks!

But wait, long-term gains to the rescue! These wise heroes are patient and smart. Hold onto your assets for over a year, and they get that special treatment - lower tax rates, my friends! It's like getting VIP access to the tax rebate club. So, cheers to long-term gains for saving us from higher taxes!

And here's a bright spot in our financial adventure - tax-exempt heroes! Federal bonds, like treasury notes, are taxed by the federal government, but they are free from state and local taxes. A tax break, my friends, like winning the lottery! Municipal bonds join the party too, saving you from excessive taxation.

So, don't despair, my F.I.R.E Starter friend! While taxable accounts may not sound thrilling at first, they do have their advantages. You can stash any amount you want in these accounts, no contribution or withdrawal limits to cramp your style. And guess what? You can access your funds during an emergency without facing any withdrawal penalties.

Why Bother With Index Funds?

Index funds strive to mimic the performance of well-known market indices like the S&P 500. They earn the "passive investment" badge because there's no fancy fund manager handpicking specific stocks and bonds. Instead, these funds excel at imitation, mirroring the market index they belong to.

Now, why do investors adore index funds so much? Well, for starters, they come with low expense ratio fees. It's a classy way of saying they won't gouge you for managing your money. The expenses are way cheaper because there's no fund manager playing the stock-picking game. It's like getting a discount coupon for your investing expenses. Index funds typically keep their fees between 0.2% and 1%, while actively managed funds often charge between 1% to 2.5%. Lower fees mean you keep more of your hard-earned money. Index funds are also adored because they offer broad market exposure and consistent returns. The final reason to adore index funds over their fancier cousins, the actively managed funds: taxes. Index funds tend to trade less frequently than actively managed funds. This results in fewer taxable events and potentially lower tax obligations for you. Cha-ching!

Dividend Reinvestment Plans (DRIPs)

So here's the deal: by reinvesting your dividend income, you not only increase the number of shares you own but also give compound interest a high-five. Automatic dividend reinvestment is a common practice. It is called the "set it and forget it" philosophy.

Setting up automatic dividend reinvestment is quite simple. Simply speak with your broker or the business that manages your index fund. They'll set you up with no issues. Many fund companies allow you to go online and set it up yourself. Once it is established, all of your lovely dividends will automatically be used to purchase additional shares of that fantastic investment that you already own.

Reinvesting dividends has now become even more interesting with the emergence of fractional shares. You don't have to hold off on purchasing a complete share until you've racked up a ton of dividends. Nope! Even a modest bit will allow you to participate.

And here's a bonus: you're also engaging in a dollar-cost averaging by continuously purchasing shares with your dividends. It resembles being an astute shopper who is aware of how to get the greatest price. You acquire shares when the market rises and when it decreases, you purchase even more.

Reinvesting your dividend profits is a no-brainer, regardless of whether you intend to hold your investment for a very long time or you're just getting started. It's similar to having a financial hidden weapon. The value of your shares will increase, compound interest will do its magic, and you'll be on your way to financial freedom before you can say "dividend reinvestment party!"

So set it and forget it, my friends, and watch your money grow like a champ while those dividends do their job. Happy investing!

Must Know Examples of Major Index Mutual Funds

Identifying index funds with the lowest expense ratio and a low minimum investment requirement is ideal. Here, we'll compare the three most prominent, and also the most affordable brokerages: Fidelity, Schwab, and Vanguard.

Fidelity

Fidelity Investments, founded in 1946, is a renowned financial services company. With its headquarters in Boston, Massachusetts, it operates as a privately-held corporation. The founding family of Fidelity are the majority owners. Fidelity's business structure is that of a diversified financial services provider, offering a wide array of investment products and services to both individual and institutional investors.

Fidelity offers a wide range of investment options, including mutual funds, index funds, exchange-traded funds (ETFs), individual stocks, bonds, and annuities. Additionally, Fidelity offers various retirement accounts like IRAs and 401(k) plans, catering to long-term financial planning and retirement needs.

While Fidelity has almost 30 index offerings I will explore the Fidelity index funds that align with a F.I.R.E. Starter plan, aiming to help you achieve your financial goals efficiently and effectively.

Fidelity Total Market Index Fund (FSKAX)

FSKAX focuses on the investment returns of a broad range of domestic stocks. This means that it invests in the 4000 companies currently listed on the stock market. 80% of its assets is allocated to the Dow Jones of which its largest holdings are as follows: 28% technology, 13% healthcare and 12% consumers. The advantage of investing in this fund over the FXAIX, which I will discuss in the next section, is the ability to invest in 4000 companies vs. 500. With such a large number of companies in its portfolio, FSKAX allows you to invest in the small and mid cap companies unlike FXAIX.

This fund aims to deliver investment outcomes that are consistent with the overall return of a wide variety of US stocks. With an expense ratio of 0.015%, this is one of the most affordable Fidelity index funds. A $1000 investment means a 15 cent annual fee. The average annual returns, as of the writing of this book last year are as follows: 1 year return of 7%, 3 year return of 14.0%, 5 year return of 12.0% and 10 year return of 11.8%.

Fidelity 500 Index Fund (FXAIX)

FXAIX, like Fidelity Total Market Index Fund, has a low expense ratio of 0.015% so that means 15 cent annual fee for every $1000 invested. At the time of this writing the returns were 9.5% for 1 year, 15.0% for 3 years, 13.0% for 5 years and 12% for 10 years.

This fund tracks the S&P 500 which is based on the 500 largest companies based on market cap. Market cap is outstanding shares multiplied by price by share. These 500 companies represent about 80% of the US market and are valued at 10 billion dollars. Keep in mind there are approximately 4000 publicly traded companies. These 500 companies make up 80% of the stock market. The fund's biggest investment sectors are 28% technology, 14% healthcare and 12% consumers.

Fidelity U.S. Bond Index Fund (FXNAX)

FXNAX bond fund aims to deliver investment outcomes that are consistent with the overall price and yield performance of the debt instruments included in the Bloomberg U.S. Aggregate Bond Index. It has approximately 8400 holdings for 590 issuers. It has a low-cost expense ratio of 0.025%, making it ideal if investors want to earn income and preserve cash. Unlike money market funds, which prioritize protecting the value of your investment, and stock funds, which seek long-term gain, bond index funds offer your portfolio the chance to generate income. Bond funds may be able to offset some of the risks that come with stock funds. These funds regularly account for inflation and invest in government bonds. At the time of this writing this fund invests 39% US Treasuries, 24% corporate bonds and 27% mortgage back securities and has 1 year return of -2.7%, 3 year return of .87%, 5 year return of 1.08% and 10 year return of 1.21%.

Fidelity Zero Funds

The Fidelity Zero Index Funds launched in 2018 and made a lot of noise in the industry because they don't have expense ratios. These are the Fidelity Zero Large Cap Index Fund (FNILX), the Fidelity Zero Extended Market Index Fund (FZIPX), the Fidelity Zero Total Market Index Fund (FZROX), and the Fidelity Zero International Index Fund (FZILX). Before we compare them, let's go through their primary goals. The FNILX tracks the U.S. large-cap index from Fidelity. This means they focus on large-cap U.S. companies by monitoring the performance of the largest 500 companies. The FZIPX mimics the performance of small and mid-cap U.S. companies, so in this case, it tracks publicly-traded U.S. companies that are not in those 500 that FNILX tracks. Finally, the FZROX combines extended market and large-cap companies and tracks 3,000 companies. If we had to compare it with other indexes, the Dow Jones U.S. Total Stock Market

Index is the closest. And lastly, the FZILX tracks Fidelity Global minus U.S. companies and follows mid-to small-cap companies overseas.

There's no denying that a zero-expense ratio has quite some appeal, but how does it compare with other paid index funds? Take a look at the chart below.

	FNILX	FZIPX	FZROX	FZILX
YTD	-13.04%	-12.96%	-13.05%	-15.93%
1-YEAR	-6.69%	-10.82%	-7.27%	-15.14%
3-YEAR	13.14%	9.08%	12.59%	3.54%

You can find affordable low cheap expense ratio index funds of course but there's a slight concern with Fidelity's zero expense ratio. They only track Fidelity's index funds, unlike other funds that are gauged against third party indexes like Center for Research in Security Prices (CRSP), Standard & Poor's (S&P), Morgan Stanley Capital International (MSCI), Russell US Indexes, and Dow Jones Industrial Average (DJAI). Do you want to invest in a fund that does not use a 3rd party indexer? To keep the expense ratio at zero many of the zero funds also invest in fewer funds unlike their counterparts that have expense ratios. FZROX has 2600 stocks but its counterpart FSKAX has 3900 or FZIPX which has 2100 versus its counterpart FSMAX which has 3700. This does not mean Zero funds are bad, it just something you should consider when deciding which funds to include in your portfolio.

Vanguard

John C. Bogle founded Vanguard Brokerage in 1975, and since then, people have associated the name 'Vanguard' with low-cost investment. With a unique business structure, it operates as a client-owned mutual fund company, meaning the investors themselves are the owners of the funds. Vanguard offers a diverse range of investment products, including 130 funds and 76 exchange-traded funds (ETFs) making it a popular choice for both individual investors and institutions seeking to grow their wealth and achieve financial independence.

Vanguard Total Stock Market Index Fund Admiral Shares (VTSAX)

VTSAX was created in 1992 and was designed to expose investors to both value and growth of U.S. equities of all market caps. It is diversified and has a low expense ratio of 0.04%. It has a minimum of $3,000 to invest. It has a 3 year return 9.67% and 10 year return 12.40%. VTSAX beats 80% of managed mutual funds. This fund is a total stock market fund so it invests in 4000 companies listed in the stock market. Total stock market funds encompass a larger portfolio of stock companies than a S&P 500 index fund. VTSAX has 4000 versus VFIAX which has 500. The presence of small cap stocks can aid the growth of a total fund like VTSAX. The fund's biggest investment sectors are 19% technology, 19% financials and 13% healthcare.

Vanguard 500 Index Fund Admiral Shares (VFIAX)

VFIAX is considered the very first index fund. It offers a diversified U.S. equity market and a low-cost expense ratio of 0.04%. It has a 3 year return of 10.18% and 10 year return of12.75%. You will need $3000 to begin investing in this fund. The top 10 companies make up 29% of the fund and remaining 490 companies make up the other 71% of VFIAX.

Vanguard Total Bond Market Index Fund Admiral Shares (VBTLX)

VBTLX fund has exposure to U.S. bonds and holds over 10,000 bonds with varying maturities giving you a broad exposure to the bond market. This index has mainly mortgage-backed securities and U.S. Treasury holdings. It has an expense ratio of 0.05%.

Vanguard Total International Stock Index Fund Admiral Shares (VTIAX)

VTIAX focuses on large foreign stocks and offers a low-cost way for investors to get exposure to emerging and developed international markets. VTIAX invests in companies outside of the U.S. It has a minimum investment of $3,000 with a 0.11% expense ratio. It invests in companies like Alibaba, HSBC, Unilever, Samsung and Shell. It has a great balance of developing and emerging markets.

Schwab

Schwab Investments, also known as Charles Schwab Corporation, was founded in 1971 by Charles R. Schwab. Schwab is a leading brokerage and financial services firm based in the United States. It is a publicly traded company. The company operates on a discount brokerage model, offering a wide range of investment products and services to individual investors and institutions.

In terms of its business structure, Schwab provides various investment offerings, including mutual funds, exchange-traded funds (ETFs), individual stocks, bonds, options, and other investment vehicles. They also offer managed accounts, retirement planning services, and access to global markets.

With a client-centric approach and a reputation for low-cost investing, Schwab aims to empower investors and provide them with the tools and resources needed to achieve their financial goals. The company's user-friendly platform and extensive research and educational materials make it appealing to both novice and experienced investors alike.

Throughout its history, Schwab has been at the forefront of innovation, embracing technology to enhance customer experience and streamline investment processes. Their commitment to transparency, reliable customer service, and a diverse range of investment options have made Schwab a popular choice for investors pursuing financial independence and early retirement.

Schwab Total Stock Market Index Fund (SWTSX)

SWTSX fund aims to track the performance of the whole U.S. market. Most of its assets are located in information technology 25.75%, followed by healthcare 14.88%. The fund comprises approximately 3400 US stock companies. It has an expense ratio of 0.03%. The top holdings are Apple, Amazon and Microsoft. The 3 year return was 8.3%, the 5 year return 10.0% and the 10 year return 12.18%.

Schwab S&P 500 Index Fund (SWPPX)

SWPPX fund intends to mirror the performance of the popular S&P 500, so it tracks some of the largest companies in the U.S. It has a lower expense ratio than the S&P 500, with just 0.02%. Like SWTSX the top holdings are Apple, Amazon and Microsoft. The 3 year return was 3 8.7%, the 5 year return 10.62% and the 10 year return 12.64%.

Schwab U.S. Aggregate Bond Index Fund (SWAGX)

SWAG is a fund that tracks U.S. Aggregate Bond Index. It has a low expense ratio of 0.04% and doesn't require a minimum investment. It comprises over 8000 bonds and it has corporate, mortgage securities and US Treasuries.

Schwab International Index Fund (SWISX)

This is Schwab's international fund, which aims to track the performance of publicly-traded and large-cap non-U.S. firms. It has a 0.06% expense ratio. This fund contains mid and large cap funds from over 20 developing markets and over 831 from countries like France and the UK. The 3 year return was 3.74%, the 5 year return was 3.01% and the 10 year return was 5.07%.

So What Now–3 Fund Portfolio Solution

So now you are familiar with the three most popular fund companies: Fidelity, Vanguard and Schwab. With the information you have about index funds, you are ready for the three fund portfolio solution. The three fund portfolio solution takes the approach that your portfolio only needs three assets: a total stock market fund, a total international fund, and a total US bond fund. This three fund approach simply states there is no need to try and beat the market with individual stocks or multiple funds when you own the market through these three fund types. With this strategy you own almost every stock and bond traded in the world. There is no overlap from these funds. Total stock fund buys USA stocks, the total international fund will buy non USA stocks and total bond fund will buy bonds securities.

Fidelity Total Market Index Fund (FSKAX), Fidelity U.S. Bond Index Fund (FXNAX), and Fidelity Total International Index Fund (FZILX) is an example of how assets are allocated in a Fidelity three-fund portfolio. Vanguard Total International Stock Index Fund (VTIAX), Vanguard Total Bond Market Index Fund (VBTLX), and Vanguard Total Stock Market Index Fund (VTSAX) is a possible option for a Vanguard three-fund portfolio. Schwab Total Stock Market Index Fund (SWTSX), Schwab U.S. Aggregate Bond Index Fund (SWAGX), and

Schwab International Index Fund (SWISX) are your options if you'd rather invest in a Schwab three-fund portfolio.

The specific allocation you choose depends on your investment objectives. You could opt for a 60% allocation to a total stock index fund, 20% to a total international fund, and 20% to a bond fund. Alternatively, you might go for a 45% allocation to a total stock index fund, 15% to a total international index fund, and 40% to a bond fund. Another option is a 50% allocation to a total stock index fund, 30% to a total international index fund, and 20% to a bond fund. These allocations can be customized based on your risk tolerance and long-term financial goals.

Target-Date Funds

When it comes to investing for retirement or your child's college education, target-date funds (TDFs) offer a compelling option. These funds are meticulously designed to align your investments with a specific time horizon. Think of them as dynamic lifecycle funds, where your investment becomes progressively more conservative as your target date approaches.

TDFs can take the form of mutual funds or exchange-traded funds (ETFs). They implement periodic rebalancing, optimizing your returns while mitigating risks according to your chosen time frame. As the target date nears, the fund automatically adjusts to a more conservative allocation, shifting a larger portion of your assets from stocks to bonds. TDFs typically mature every five years, such as in 2015, 2020, and 2025, but one drawback is that they often come with relatively high expense ratios.

Advantages of Target-Date Funds (TDFs)

Imagine you're a savvy investor with a 401(k) who doesn't relish the idea of painstakingly selecting and managing various investments in your portfolio. TDFs come to your rescue, sparing you from decision paralysis. To harness the power of these financial wizards, all you need to do is choose a TDF that matches your intended retirement horizon, and voilà! You're good to go. Once you've made your selection, the fund managers take over, handling all the intricate asset management and rebalancing tasks on your behalf.

Now, here's the secret sauce: some experts even recommend sticking with a single TDF. Why, you ask? Well, they believe that you can achieve your financial goals without the hassle of juggling multiple funds. It's like finding the ultimate investment autopilot. Simply chart your course with a single TDF, sit back, and watch it work its magic. It's akin to having a dependable co-pilot who knows precisely how to steer you toward your destination.

Let's not forget why 401(k) investors adore these TDFs so much. They provide a convenient one-stop-shop solution, sparing you the headache of managing a complex portfolio. No need to fret over a multitude of investment options when you can have confidence in just one TDF. It's akin to having a superhero sidekick who makes managing your money a breeze.

So, fellow investor, while my personal preference leans toward index funds due to their typically lower expense ratios and market-tracking abilities, if you're in search of an investment strategy as simple as apple pie, TDFs might be the answer. Just remember, it's always wise to conduct your research and fully comprehend any investment before committing. With the right approach, you'll be well on your way to financial independence and early retirement!

Disadvantages of Target-Date Funds (TDFs)

One potential drawback of TDFs stems from their frequent asset reallocation, due to active management. While the idea of having your investments expertly handled may sound appealing, it can clash with your specific investing style because active trading often leads to higher expense ratios. The more you spend on fees, the less your investments have available to work toward your financial objectives.

Consider a scenario where you initially plan to retire at a specific age, but unforeseen circumstances prompt you to retire earlier or extend your working years. TDFs lack the ability to predict and adapt to such changes, highlighting the importance of maintaining flexibility and adjusting your investment strategy accordingly.

But that's not all! The absence of a guarantee that TDFs will outpace inflation or generate the returns necessary to meet your objectives looms as the biggest risk. Entering the battlefield without armor can be unsettling. TDFs can also be costly, further exacerbating the issue. Comprising multiple underlying funds, they come with a high price tag. Each of these funds carries its expense ratio, and on top of that, the TDF itself charges an administrative fee. This can take a toll on your wallet.

Therefore, as you embark on your financial journey, keep these considerations in mind. Despite their limitations, TDFs can still be a valuable tool in your quest for financial independence and early retirement. Just remember to weigh their costs against potential benefits and maintain vigilant oversight of your investments. With a mix of prudence and adventure, you'll navigate the investment landscape like a seasoned pro.

Exchange-Traded Funds (ETFs)

Alright, my financial adventurers! Gather 'round and let's explore the world of ETFs. Now, ETF may seem like a strange code to you, but do not worry! I'm here to translate it for you.

Imagine this: ETFs resemble individual stocks but behave like index funds. ETFs collect a variety of assets into one pool, just like mutual funds do but the twist is that you can trade ETFs like stocks throughout a trading day, unlike traditional funds where trades take place at 4PM, which is close of the trading day. It's like getting the freedom of stocks and the diversity of index funds in one package! ETFs give investors the ability to time when they purchase and sell investments. ETFs like their counterparts index funds are a low cost way to achieve diversification. ETFs are becoming popular with investors because unlike many index funds they do not have a minimum investment requirement and the expense ratios tend to be a bit lower than index funds.

Mutual Funds vs. Index Funds vs. ETFs–Which Should You Choose

Now that you know what mutual funds, index funds, and ETFs are, how do you determine which one might be more beneficial for your goals than the others? Remember that all three allow you to make an investment and own all the underlying stocks that make up the mutual fund, the index fund or the ETF. This one trade gives you diversification unlike purchasing one stock. Mutual funds are professionally managed with an active fund manager with usually 1-2% expense ratio. These high expense ratios will eat into your over portfolio growth over time.

Index funds operate without an active fund manager, adhering to a passive investment strategy. They mirror the risk of the underlying market, such as the S&P 500 or Dow

Jones Industrial Average. This approach typically outperforms the majority of actively managed mutual funds.

ETFs, like mutual funds and index funds, are composed of many stock companies. You can buy and sell an ETF on the market unlike mutual and index funds. Some ETFs now allow you to purchase fractional shares.

Now that recap is over, which should you choose? Many who are advocates of F.I.R.E choose index funds over mutual funds and ETFs. Index funds allow you to do automated investing unlike its cousins the ETF. You do not have to find time to put a buy order in for an index fund like you do with an ETF. Index funds also allow you to have investment vehicles with the lowest expense ratios, unlike mutual funds.

P.S. Keep in mind that, despite the fact that I am a mere mortal with access to all available investing knowledge, I am unable to foresee the future. Therefore, use my advice with caution and always conduct your own research. Invest wisely!

Robo-Advisors vs. Full-Service Brokerages vs. Discount Brokers

Choosing a broker is essential to match your investing style and overall goals. Nowadays, many options exist for choosing a broker that fits your style. In this section, I'll go through some of the main characteristics of the different brokers you can choose from. There are two main categories for brokers: discount brokers and full-service. Discount brokers usually work as an intermediary to larger brokers, offering a less complicated system designed for new investors. In contrast, full service brokers can deal directly with you.

Regardless of your choice, all brokers are, in some capacity, intermediaries between you and stock exchanges. You will always have a broker because the exchange only allows assets to be sold and bought if you are a member of that exchange, so you'll always need someone to trade in your place. Because most brokers provide that service for you, they usually get paid through commissions.

Full-Service vs. Discount Brokers

The full-service: think of them as an all-inclusive glitzy package. They provide you investment options and saturate you with personalized advice. It's like having a personal money expert at your side, but this opulent service may cost you.

The discount brokers are the outlaws of the brokerage industry, on the other hand. They enable you to make independent investing decisions without going over budget. It's like entering a buffet where you may select your favorite financial treats. Just be aware that these brokers might not provide the same level of personalized attention or high-end guidance as their full-service rivals. WeBull, Robinhood and M1 Finance are examples of discount brokers.

The key to selecting the ideal broker for your investing style is is this: brokers with low commissions are your best friends. They won't drain your bank account. On the other hand, zero-commission brokers are the way to go if you're a trading lunatic who enjoys switching between investments more quickly than an over-caffeinated kangaroo.

Do your research before selecting a broker. Verify that they meet the necessary requirements, such as are they are a registered investment advisor (RIA). Being a RIA means there are a few essential requirements that a broker must fulfill with the Securities and Exchange Commission (SEC) before being licensed. The SEC is the regulatory watchdog. This posh body ought to regulate the broker you've chosen. You could compare it to a financial guardian angel keeping an eye on your investments. They ensure that everyone is abiding by the regulations and maintain control over the financial sector.

Before you choose a broker to go on your financial journey with you confirm that they have this formal endorsement and if it is possible make sure the people you are dealing with are honest and knowledgeable.

Don't forget about FINRA, the Financial Industry Regulatory Authority. Many brokers have this designation well. The FINRA oversee fair play and uphold order in the sector, acting as the referees in the financial game. Therefore, confirm that FINRA has registered your broker. Without a dependable sheriff, you wouldn't want to be left all alone in the lawless financial west, would you?

Go forth and rule the world of investing now that you're equipped with understanding the different types of brokerages. Do your homework, weigh your possibilities, and select the option that, like a good pair of shoes, fits your investment style.

Robo-Advisors

Robo-advisors are the high-tech magicians of the financial world. These automated platforms are similar to the cool, geeky pals that build and manage your investing account using sophisticated algorithms. However, some of them do have actual people working behind the scenes, just in case you need a human touch. They are all about efficiency and minimizing human interaction. Wealthfront, Betterment and Acorns are examples of Robo Advisors.

It's just as simple to sign up for a robo-advisor as ordering pizza online, albeit without the delectable toppings. You visit their website and respond to a number of questions regarding your investment objectives, risk tolerance, and time horizon.

It's similar to being questioned about your financial goals by a financial advisor. Once you provide your answers, the robo-advisor gets to work creating a portfolio specifically for you.

Let's now discuss the benefits of these robotic wonders. Cost, in one word. Robo-advisors pass on the savings to you because they reduce the need for human intervention. You'll pay between 0.02% and 1% of your investment per year, which is a tiny fraction of what you'd spend for a traditional broker.

The catch is that robo-advisors have some restrictions. These automated maestros will build your portfolio using these pre-selected options and are great admirers of ETFs. Therefore, you might want to look at other options if you want a more customized approach to your investments.

As you begin your F.I.R.E. Starter plan remember that picking a broker doesn't require a lifetime commitment either. Your financial goals may change as you go along because life is all about growth and change. So, when the moment is right, don't be hesitant to change things up and investigate different brokerage accounts.

Therefore, whether you're working with a robo-advisor, a discount or full service broker, or a combination of all, have an open mind, stay informed, and adjust to the investment environment's constant ebbs and flow.

Tax-Efficient Accounts

Taxes are an exciting subject! Even the most courageous investors can shudder at the mere mention of taxes, I know. But don't worry, since tax-efficient accounts are here to save the day and assist you in achieving early retirement and financial independence.

Imagine yourself on a mission to increase your fortune. Along the road, you run against numerous costs, including irksome taxes and expense ratios. When this happens, tax-efficient accounts swoop in to save you from Uncle Sam's grasp. These accounts act as magical shields that reduce your tax liability compared to conventional accounts. And let me tell you, these accounts are a game-changer when it comes to retiring early, especially if you find yourself in the high echelons of higher tax brackets.

Now, if you work a job for an organization, chances are good that you already know about some of these tax-efficient accounts. You may be familiar with the legendary individual retirement account also known as an IRA or the powerful 401(k). Your hard-earned money can find refuge in these accounts, protected, to some degree from undue taxation. Keep in mind they have restrictions. Yes, the government likes to keep an eye on things and establishes a cap on the annual contributions that can be made to these accounts. It acts as a kind of financial speed restriction.

You might wonder why you should be concerned about tax-efficient investing in these enchanted accounts. You should be concerned because they hold the secret to boosting your long-term gains. Yes, diversifying your portfolio and choosing tax efficient investments are crucial, because they often delay you from having to pay taxes when you're in a high income tax bracket. Tax efficient investment accounts prevent taxes from sneaking up and grabbing a portion of your hard earned investment growth.

Types of Tax-Efficient and Tax-Advantage Accounts

There are two main tax-efficient accounts: 401(k) and Individual Retirement Account (IRA).

401(k) Account

Ah, the enigmatic world of 401(k)s! 401(k)s resembles a covert savings strategy intended to enable you to enjoy a comfortable retirement while playing the tax game. So let's try to solve this mystery.

Imagine that you are a diligent worker in the good ol' USA. Your employer approaches you with a suggestion: invest your retirement money in a 401(k). You consent to deposit a specific proportion of your monthly salary into this enchanted investing account. Then you find out that your employer can match your investment by a stated percentage like 4%! Your investment has made money even before it is invested because of the employers match. The money is taken from your check pre-tax. Taxes are paid when you reach the age of retirement and begin withdrawing money. The belief is that during retirement, you should be in a lower income bracket then when you were employed, so the rate of taxation should be lower.

Many employers now offer a 401(k) plan that offers conventional and Roth investing. With the conventional method, your contributions are subtracted from your income before taxes, lowering your taxable income. But keep in mind, like I said earlier, the taxman will knock on your door when you ultimately retire and wish to withdraw the money.

The Roth 401(k) is a new employer retirement offering. This guy accepts investments post-tax employment check, so you do not receive an immediate tax reduction in your paycheck. The real kicker, though, is that you may bid the taxman farewell after you retire. With the Roth 401(k), unlike the traditional 401(k), you paid taxes on the money going in so you do not have to pay taxes when you are ready to withdraw your money.

Not all employers provide the Roth option. Just keep in mind that there are yearly contributions caps set by the IRS. For those under 50 in 2022, it was $20,500, and if you were fortunate enough to be 50 or older, you received an additional $6,500. A generous company might even match your contributions.

The real fun will now start when you select the funds for your 401(k). Your choice of investments and the amount of contributions you make can have a huge impact. Your hidden weapon is time, my friend. The sooner you begin, the longer you have to see your money grow. It's the compounding power, baby! Reinvest those profits, allow them to compound, and see your retirement savings grow.

But be patient, my eager investor! Money withdrawals from your 401(k) can be a little challenging. Naturally, Uncle Sam wants his share. Taxes will become an issue once you begin taking withdrawals at age 59½ or older. Ouch! If your 401(k) offers a Roth component you will be able to take qualified withdrawals tax free after age 59 ½. If you take money out of your 401(k) plan before age 59½ you will face a 10% early withdrawal penalty. And just when you believed you were safe, the "required minimum distribution" (RMD) comes into play. You'll have to start withdrawing funds from the 401(k) once you turn 72.

Individual Retirement Accounts (IRA)

An IRA, often called a traditional individual retirement account, is a retirement account that allows you to postpone paying taxes on the growth until you withdraw the money at 591/2 or older. Similar to a 401(k), but with your choice and management of the account as opposed to your employer managing the account. IRAs are frequently used by investors as one of their means of retirement savings. Even people who have access to employer-sponsored plans like a 401(k) or 403(b) can still take advantage of IRA tax advantages to increase their savings and provide their portfolio more flexibility. There are several types of IRAs: Roth, SEP, and SIMPLE. Each type has its own set of rules and regulations regarding eligibility, taxation, and withdrawals.

SEP and SIMPLE IRAs are the IRA crew's cool youngsters. Both resemble a 401(k) in that they are established by the employer. Small employers will often offer Simplified Employee Pension (SEP) IRAs as a possible retirement vehicle. It allows the employer to set up IRAs and contribute to the employee's retirement. Employees are not allowed to contribute. SIMPLE IRAs allow both the employer and employee to contribute funds to the employees retirement account. Both SEP and SIMPLE IRAs allow the employer to contribute large sums to an employee's retirement account

Roth IRA is a type of retirement account. You won't pay taxes on the potential growth of your funds with a Roth IRA account, and you'll be able to take tax-free withdrawals at age 591/2 after the account has been open for five years. If you anticipate being in a higher tax band in the future, a Roth IRA may be a useful way to save money because tax-free distributions are an added benefit. Not everyone will qualify for a Roth IRA, though, as there are income restrictions for starting one. There is also no required minimum distribution.

So, my friend, whether you have a regular 401(k) or one that includes a 401(k) Roth, SEP, or SIMPLE IRA, the goal is to save money for your retirement.

Backdoor Roth IRA

If your income is too high to contribute to a Roth IRA, there is another legal way to contribute to a Roth IRA and get the advantages of tax free withdrawals. You can make a contribution to a traditional IRA and later convert it to a Roth rather than making a straight contribution to a Roth. This is a legal workaround for the income restrictions that typically preclude high earners from establishing Roth IRAs. Although the backdoor Roth IRA technique may result in higher taxes when it is first implemented, you will still receive the long-term tax benefits of a Roth account. Even though this backdoor technique results in higher tax gains in the year you make the conversion knowing that your money can be taken out tax free during retirement is heart warming.

Smart Estate Planning With Roth IRAs

Ah, estate planning—the fascinating realm of lowering your tax liability after death! It's similar to playing a game of financial chess where you plan your moves to avoid leaving your loved ones with a big tax bill but yet leaving a legacy. And what's this? The star players in this elaborate plan are Roth IRAs.

The money you leave your heirs in a Roth IRA doesn't have to go through the probate court system, just like the assets from a traditional retirement account or a life insurance policy. The named beneficiaries can take distributions for themselves for 10 years if the account was open for at least five years. Your spouse can inherit the account as if they were the original holder of the account and spread distributions over their life time. Your beneficiaries are not required to take minimum distributions from a Roth IRA, in contrast to conventional retirement plans.

The true show-stopper is right here: Your Roth IRA can be passed on to your heirs tax-free because you've already paid taxes on it. Giving them a golden goose that produces tax-free eggs would be analogous. What a legacy that never stops giving!

Totally Legal Examples of Legal Tax Avoidance Strategies

Tax avoidance—the skill that allows you to pay less in taxes without inciting the taxman's fury! Let's explore the wonderful world of tax avoidance, where we'll concentrate on the ethical methods rather than the dubious ones that could get you into trouble. For those brave individuals who love living on the edge, we'll leave tax evasion to them but not in this book, folks!

Visualize this: You're an intelligent taxpayer, and you want to keep your money in your wallet. Embracing the mysterious world of deductions and credits is one approach to accomplish this. It resembles having a private armory of tools to combat taxes. You go deeply into the trove of deductions and list every allowable item you come across. The standard deduction is now your dependable companion on your journey. It's like a magical shield that makes it easy for you to lower your taxable income. In 2021, it will be a swanky $12,950 for people. But hey, the deduction doubles to a whooping $25,900 if you're happily married. It's similar to receiving a covert tax break from the government. Finding every piece of information that can help you reduce your tax liability makes you feel like a modern-day Sherlock Holmes. Don't overlook the wonderful credits either, which miraculously reduce your tax liability. It's as if you could wave a wand and have your tax bill vanish into thin air. Poof!

There's still more, though! The world of investing in tax-advantaged accounts like 401(k), 403(b), IRA and Roth IRAs beckons. You have the ability to protect your money from taxation by directing your money into these accounts. During retirement you will have to pay taxes on 401(k), 403(b) and IRA withdrawals. Like I said, earlier, the thought here is that you will be in a lower income bracket so the taxes should be lower than when you were working. Roth IRA contributions were taxed before being invested so the money taken out can be tax free.

Then there are tax avoidance benefits from mortgages. If you have a mortgage you can get a tax deduction! As you work toward your goal of becoming a homeowner, keep this tax deduction in mind because it's like a secret path that takes you to lower taxes. Armed with your deductions for mortgage interest, you march boldly into the land of deductions and legal tax avoidance.

Oh, and don't forget about the child tax credit, a champion of family budgets. It acts as a barrier to guard your wallet from the tax dragon's flaming breath. With every qualified child you have, you strengthen your defenses, lowering your tax obligations and providing a better future for your children. How about a win-win scenario?

Finally, there is the venerable health savings account, a victor in the fight against medical costs. It's similar to a magic elixir that lowers your pre-tax income and enables you to save money for medical expenses. If you do not use the money in your HSA the money would roll over year after year. At age 65 if you have money in your HSA, you are able to take the money out for non-medical expenses, penalty, free, but keep in mind, you still will have to pay ordinary income tax.

Let's now dispel any misunderstandings. Let's define the difference between tax evasion and tax avoidance. Tax evasion is the shadowy side that we must not do at all costs; tax avoidance is our noble goal. As you can see, dear taxpayer, tax evasion entails concealing income, acting as though you didn't make a penny, or snatching up credits that aren't legally yours. That's like trying to scam the tax collector, but believe me, that won't work out well. Tax evasion is a severe crime, and as a not-so-welcome bonus, you may be subject to steep fines or even a warm jail cell. Let's keep our noses clean and stay on the good side of Uncle Sam, shall we?

Remember, my fellow tax-savvy explorer, that the goal is to follow the laws, take advantage of tax-advantaged accounts, and maximize your deductions.

Now raise a glass in a toast to your genius tax-saving and estate plan. Cheers to your prosperity and generational wealth plan!

Social Security Payments

There is a good probability that you have been contributing to the Social Security system like a responsible citizen during your working life.

You can go to the Social Security Administration's website and sign up for an account in the manner of a tech-savvy future retiree in order to learn the ins and outs of your Social Security income. You'll find their handy calculators there, which can give you an accurate estimate of how much money you will receive in retirement. It is almost as if you had a personal digital accountant who was working for you, calculating the figures to disclose the overall sum.

But hold on, there's more to it! You can act like a retiree on a mission by walking right into a Social Security Administration office. They will assist you in calculating what is legitimately yours.

Delayed Retirement Credits

Delayed Retirement Credits are a little-known weapon that you can use in your arsenal when it comes time to retirement. If you opt to play the waiting game with your retirement benefits, the Social Security Administration will bestow upon you what is essentially a greater payout. From the time you reach your full retirement age until the age of 70, the Social Security Administration will reward you with raises at a rate of around two-thirds of one percent per month, on average.

Remember, my future retiree extraordinaire, that Social Security payments aren't guaranteed, but you can maximize what the Social Security Administration owes you by practicing cautious planning and taking advantage of as many delayed retirement credits as possible.

What are Capital Gains?

The sweet satisfaction of generating money by selling your investments for more than you bought it for is known as capital gains. It's the equivalent of earning a perfect score for your investment prowess. You see, the magic of capital gains happens when you sell any of your fancy assets like stocks, investment funds or property and make a profit.

Now, calm down, my enthusiastic investor friend, there are two types of capital gains: short-term and long-term. Both have their advantages and disadvantages. Profits from the sale of an asset that you've owned for less than a year are subject to short-term capital gains tax. According to your tax bracket, which ranges from 10% to 37%, short-term capital gains taxes are paid at the same rate as you'd pay on your ordinary income.

The tax known as long-term capital gains tax is levied on assets held for more than a year. Depending on your income, the long-term capital gains tax rates are 0%, 15%, and 20%.

Now, if you've ever dabbled in the world of mutual funds, you know how important it is to know when you'll be collecting those gains and when the taxman will come knocking on your door. During the course of the year, mutual funds accumulate their gains in a manner analogous to that of a squirrel storing nuts. They wait until the very last moment of the year to make the distribution of those earnings to their most devoted holders, that would be you! It's kind of like getting a gift that you didn't expect at the end of the year. But hold on, there's going to be some paperwork involved. When doing your taxes, you are required to file a form known as a 1099-DIV and declare the amount of earnings you have earned along with the type of gains, regardless of whether they are short-term or long-term gains.

Dividend Income

Dividends are similar to receiving a small bonus from the businesses you invest in. They serve as a tasty reward that enhances the enjoyment of investment. So, my financially savvy friend, here is the lowdown on dividends.

Imagine you own some expensive stocks and the firms decide to give you a portion of their profits. They are saying, "hey, we appreciate your faith in us! We will give you a piece of the pie." The company's board of directors typically decides on the dividend amount. They act as the final arbiters, but rather than wearing regal robes, they dress in suits and ties.

Let's now discuss frequency. Most payouts arrive on schedule every three months. It is like a dependable friend who visits every three months bearing gifts. However, there are a few rebels about. Some businesses make dividend payments every month. It appears as though they are eager to give you the profits they have earned.

Now, if you're a math freak, you may have heard the term "dividend yield." Although it may sound elegant, it is simply a method of calculating the dividend per share and expressing it as a percentage. It resembles the stock exercising its dividend muscles. In connection to the stock price, the bigger the proportion, the more goods you'll receive.

But hold on, this dividend celebration has a schedule. The "ex-dividend date" is a certain day before businesses begin to sprinkle their dividend magic. It resembles a party invitation. You can participate as long as you possess the shares on that date. Like a distinguished visitor, you are prepared to claim your dividend award. Mark the date on your calendar and get ready to party.

Here's a little-known fact: not all businesses participate in the dividend game. Some of them, like those egotistical siblings who don't want to share their toys, want to keep their earnings to themselves. They instead put those profits back into the business. They seem to be implying, "Sorry, no dividends for you, but we're cooking up something big here!" So be sure to choose stocks from the kind company that shares its profits with you if you're seeking those dividend treats. Yum!

Let's discuss the sectors that are reputed to be more dividend-friendly while we're on the subject of bountiful bunches. We're referring to the banking and finance crowd, the pharmaceutical gang, the utility crew, and the primary material group. They share their profits with their devoted stockholders like the cool kids do. These are the sectors to watch if you want to hang out with the dividend party animals.

Never forget, my friend, that adding dividends to your investing portfolio can be a delectable move. It serves as the icing on your financial dessert. Just be sure to perform your research, comprehend the businesses you're investing in, and take pleasure in the benefits they bestow upon you. Happy investment, and may you always reap the rewards!

Dividend Tax Rates

Dividend taxes and their fascinating world! Prepare for an exhilarating voyage through the world of numbers and tax brackets. Are you prepared? Let's start now!

The qualifying and the regular ordinary dividend taxes are the two sorts of dividend taxes that you, my financial buddy, should be aware of.

Ordinary dividends are held for less than 60 days and are taxed at income rates.

Qualified dividends are dividends held for 60 days in the 121 day period before the ex-dividend date and the Qualified dividend tax rates are correlated with the capital gains tax rate. It appears that they are working together to reduce your taxes with the earnings. Sneaky, yes? Depending on your income level, these qualifying dividends may be subject to a tax rate of 0%, 15%, or 20%.

Here is a handy table that shows the eligible dividend tax rates for each filing status for the year 2022: single filers, heads of households, married individuals filing jointly, and individuals who wish to file separately. You can use it as a cheat sheet to get around the confusing dividend tax system. Isn't that considerate?

SINGLE FILERS

TAX RATE	TAXABLE INCOME BRACKET
0%	FROM $0 TO $41,675
15%	FROM $41,676 TO $459,750
20%	FROM $445,851

HEAD OF HOUSEHOLD

TAX RATE	TAXABLE INCOME BRACKET
0%	FROM $0 TO $55,800
15%	FROM $55,801 TO $488,500
20%	FROM $488,501

MARRIED (JOINTLY)

TAX RATE	TAXABLE INCOME BRACKET
0%	FROM $0 TO $83,350
15%	FROM $83,351 TO $517,200
20%	FROM $517,201

MARRIED (SEPARATELY)	
TAX RATE	TAXABLE INCOME BRACKET
0%	FROM $0 TO $41,675
15%	FROM $41,676 TO $258,600
20%	FROM $258,601

Building the Perfect Portfolio For Your Goals

The exciting journey that is portfolio construction! As we explore the fascinating world of stocks, bonds, and all things monetary, get ready for some financial fun. Have you prepared? Lets rock and roll, then!

Therefore, an investment portfolio is like your team of financial superheroes, my fellow ambitious investor. It is a compilation of all of your assets, including mutual funds, equities, ETFs, and anything else in between. Imagine it as your own Avengers squad, only they won't be saving the planet; instead, they'll be assisting you in reaching your financial objectives. Amazing, isn't that?

Let's now discuss danger. It is comparable to the financial world's roller coaster. While some people enjoy the rush, others would rather have their feet firmly planted. Your risk tolerance should be taken into account when constructing your portfolio. It's similar to figuring out how many pulse-pounding loops and twists you can take before losing your lunch. Finding that sweet spot where you can take the risks and yet stand a chance of making some money is key.

But do not worry, dear investor friend! You don't have to go through this crazy adventure by yourself if you still do not feel ready after reading this book. Remember, you can get assistance from robo-advisors, discount and full service brokerage companies. They will lead you with their knowledge and experience, acting as the Yodas of the financial world. If you do not feel comfortable charting the waters on your own, they all have financial advisors and a slew of information to help you in, selecting the right investments. They aid you with building a portfolio that includes and considers IRAs, 401(k)s, Roth 401(k)s, and other investment vehicles.

Let's now discuss the investments themselves, which make up your portfolio's main attractions. It's comparable to picking the ideal cast for a big-budget film. Stocks are available, which can be riskier but also more lucrative. Bonds provide security and a set income, much like the dependable supporting performers. Then there are index funds and mutual funds, which are like the supporting cast and offer you a bit of everything. The crucial word here is diversification. It's like having a large cast of various personalities, all of whom add something special to the big screen.

However, there's still more! It's important to decide how to allocate your assets. It's similar to deciding how much time each performer spends on screen. To maximize returns and reduce risks, you want to maintain a balance between your assets. There are also "rules" that advise how much you should devote to various assets, such as the "100 minus your age rule". It's similar to following a script to guarantee a successful performance. Just keep in mind that these principles can be adjusted to meet your particular style and financial objectives.

Regarding styles, there are a variety of investment portfolios to fit your preferences. There are risk-taking aggressive portfolios, adventurous moderate portfolios, and conservative portfolios. It's similar to choosing your movie's genre. You can choose the portfolio that best suits your desire for excitement: high-risk or low-risk investments or a unique blend of both.

So, with information, build your ideal team of assets, enjoy the highs and lows of investing, and may your portfolio be the big financial success of your life.

Generational Wealth

When we discuss generational wealth, we're referring to the possessions that are passed down within a single family from one generation to the next. It resembles a game of financial hot potato in which assets like real estate, stocks, companies, and cash are included. This wealth transfer can be split into two groups: "after death" and "during life." For the typical family, the first category, sometimes referred to as a "inheritance," is typically quite modest. In fact, the average inheritance between 1996 and 2016 was close to $50,000. In some places, the inheritance may be subject to taxation after it reaches a certain level, typically in the form of an inheritance or estate tax. You might be asking, "What's the difference?" at this point. Well, the estate tax is paid by the estate itself, whereas the inheritance tax is often paid by the fortunate heirs who inherit the assets. Only when the transfer of wealth exceeds a predetermined threshold, which in 2022 was $12.06 million, do these taxes become applicable.

A person's lifetime can also be used to transfer generational wealth, but in such cases, be ready to pay more in taxes. Giving presents is the most typical way that wealth is transferred during life. This frequently occurs, for instance, when the family's children require assistance with a down payment for a piece of real estate. There are additional ways to transfer wealth. For instance, paying for someone's schooling might be a kind gesture that is also tax-exempt.

Receiving an inheritance or gifts might give your F.I.R.E. journey a huge boost. Just keep in mind to invest carefully or use the money sensibly if you happen to receive a nice lump sum. That is the formula for quickening your financial progress. People who are lucky enough to inherit wealth from previous generations frequently have better financial circumstances than those who do not. They maybe able to escape the terrible student loan and credit card debt that plague so many. They might even utilize the bequest to buy assets like real estate, which would boost their fortune even further.

You now have all the necessary knowledge about generational wealth to make wise decisions and maximize your F.I.R.E. Starter plan!

Chapter 6: How to Set Yourself on F.I.R.E. – Starter Types for Retiring Early

Financial independence has a broad definition. The definition most people relate to is having enough wealth to live a comfortable life without the need to work but it can also mean meeting one's financial obligation and still being able to save money at the end of the month. There are these two interpretations of the term F.I.R.E. and there's a myriad of others that would be just as suitable.

For example, the baby boomer generation didn't do a great job preparing for their future. For people aged 56 to 61, the average amount of money in their retirement account is $25,000.

Having so little saved and invested is also one of the reasons there are different definitions of F.I.R.E. So in this last chapter, I'll discuss the different types of F.I.R.E. and how each has its benefits while still being able to suit your lifestyle.

Getting Fat With F.I.R.E.

The mysterious Fat F.I.R.E. It's like finding the secret to early retirement; it's the stuff of legends. Fat F.I.R.E. is when you live a luxurious lifestyle and retire early. Throughout your retirement, you should be able to spend comfortably and lavishly during each year of retirement. Fat F.I.R.E. assumes you'll be making at least $200,000 a year in retirement, so high income earners or business owners are more likely to achieve this type of F.I.R.E. because to support the lifestyle,

"Fat F.I.R.E." requires for substantially greater savings and investing. Fat F.I.R.E. means your investment income more than covers your best life's living expenditures. You can comfortably subsist without a job. You don't require any additional work or activities in your life. Additionally, if you are Fat F.I.R.E., you may live in some of the most beautiful cities on earth without having to worry about money.

Going on a Diet – Lean F.I.R.E.

Lean the hidden weapon of the thrifty. These thrifty friends of F.I.R.E. are experts at making ends meet! Lean F.I.R.E. is the key to financial independence and retirement at warp speed if you're prepared to tighten your purse strings and make every dollar count. Prepare to let your inner money-saving ninja loose and enjoy the benefits!

The fact that Lean F.I.R.E. caters to those of us with limited resources is one of its greatest advantages. This method will have you dancing your way to financial freedom in no time if you have a talent for getting every last penny out of your paycheck. Who doesn't want to retire early and live a good life, after all?

Lean F.I.R.E. is when someone spends less annually than the typical consumer and has saved up 25 times their annual costs, which, like we discussed earlier is the standard threshold for financial independence. Lean F.I.R.E. refers to the ability to retire earlier than the typical age of 65 with an extremely frugal and basic lifestyle. Lean F.I.R.E. suggests that you are only investing enough to pay for your bare minimum expenses, such as food, transportation, and rent. There isn't much room for extravagance. Lean F.I.R.E. differs from the Fat F.I.R.E. lifestyle in that it lays a heavy emphasis on being thrifty. To achieve Lean F.I.R.E and have your annual expenses covered in retirement a frugal lifestyle is required. Living a lean F.I.R.E. lifestyle entails working hard to save and invest. This may entail giving up some of life's luxuries in order to save and invest enough money to support an early retirement.

Barista F.I.R.E. And Why It Has Nothing To Do With Coffee

Barista F.I.R.E. is the world's most hybrid rebel! It falls somewhere between Fat F.I.R.E. and Lean F.I.R.E. This method is your saving grace if you don't want to toil away at a 9 to 5 job until you have saved a million dollars. You can experience a comfortable early retirement and the sweet taste of financial independence with Barista F.I.R.E.

Barista F.I.R.E. is the ability to retire earlier than the typical age of 65 while working a part-time job for extra money and if you live in the United States for health insurance. The core strategy focuses on aggressively saving and investing, as well as producing passive income through investments and side hustles. The objective is to build up enough wealth to support your lifestyle and become financially independent when you are still relatively young. The Barista F.I.R.E technique places a similar emphasis on saving a sizable amount of your income as does classic Lean F.I.R.E. Depending on your objectives and time frame, the precise savings rate may change, but in general, you should save at least 25% to 30% or more of your income. Those following the Barista F.I.R.E. Starter plan typically live for the day they have just enough money to say take this job and shove it.

Is Barista F.I.R.E. calling your name? Are you ready to design your own path and flip the script on traditional retirement? If so, bid adieu to the arduous goal of saving $1,000,000 and welcome to a future that is more adaptable, fulfilling, and financially independent. You can enjoy life with one side hustle. Prepare to revolutionize Barista F.I.R.E. and experience the liberation you've always desired. Let the thrilling new chapter of your life begin. The voyage is waiting!

Coast F.I.R.E.

Coast F.I.R.E. refers to the practice of riding the wave of investments and letting them handle the labor-intensive tasks while you relax and take advantage of beach life. That's the kind of retirement strategy I prefer!

Financial independence is a goal of Coast F.I.R.E. You've saved enough money in your retirement accounts at this point to coast through retirement. Your account contributions do not have to be increased. Instead, you can let time and compound interest work their magic.

The term "retire early" isn't often used when referring to Coast F.I.R.E. Compared to the requirements of the original F.I.R.E. movement, it is less demanding. When an individual reaches Coast F.I.R.E., they frequently continue working until their late 50s or early 60s but stop contributing to their retirement funds at the age of 50. Instead of retiring early as in traditional F.I.R.E., the goal is to save and invest earlier in life so that compound interest and investment returns coasts you towards financial independence in your senior years.

Conclusion

So, my fellow financial explorers, we have arrived at the conclusion of our F.I.R.E. Starter tour. Hasn't it been quite the journey?

To recap what we learned about how to budget? Ah, the excitement of doing the math and understanding that spending must drastically decrease. Reducing spending and paying down debt is the path to F.I.R.E. It may feel like attempting to tame a wild animal, but hey, it's necessary for the life of financial freedom. Accept the challenge. I believe in you!

Let's not forget about the emergency fund, which serves as a financial superpower. When life throws you a curveball, it's your safety net, your protector, and the reason you won't have to sell your kidney on the underground market. Oh, and don't forget life insurance—for those occasions in which you must ensure that your loved ones are cared for, even from the great beyond.

But wait, there's still more! The secret to your financial kingdom can be found in the magic formula of The 25% Rule, which you must never lose sight of. There are numerous F.I.R.E. calculators available online and waiting to crunch the numbers for you. Save time by letting the calculators handle the laborious computations while you sip your coffee and daydream about sunny beaches.

The craft of goal-setting is up next. F.I.R.E. is about early retirement, but that doesn't imply you need to live in a cave like a hermit. No, you can still take pleasure in life's finer things. You can have these pleasures by adding them to, set short-term, mid-term, and long-term goals.

And now, my fellow explorers, we have reached the climax of your F.I.R.E. Starter journey—the grand finale. My friend, now is the moment to invest and let your money do its magic! Available are a variety of investment choices: from tax-efficient accounts to portfolio diversification. Watch your riches increase like a garden that has been well-tended to, and savor the pleasant taste of your monetary achievement.

So let's raise a glass to the effort, sacrifice, and unshakable commitment it takes to seek your fairy tale ending as we say goodbye to this epic narrative of financial independence and early retirement. Although F.I.R.E. is not for the weak of heart, the rewards at the finish line are incredible! Keep saving, dreaming, and keeping your sights set on the goal. Your autonomous, stress-free early retirement is waiting for you. Salutations, my fellow F.I.R.E. Starter!

A F.I.R.E. Starter Music Playlist

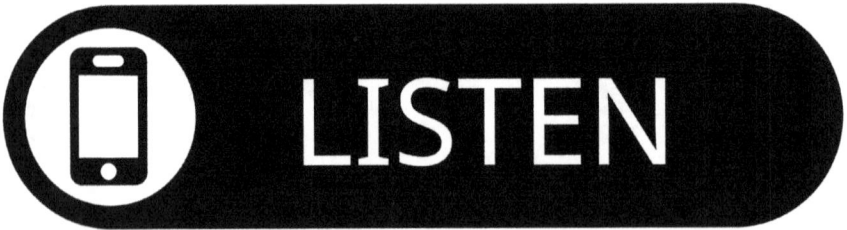

LISTEN

Follow Us TikTok

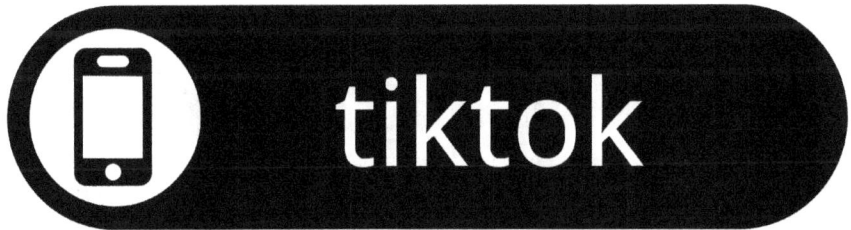

tiktok

Follow Us Instagram

Free Beneficiary Planner

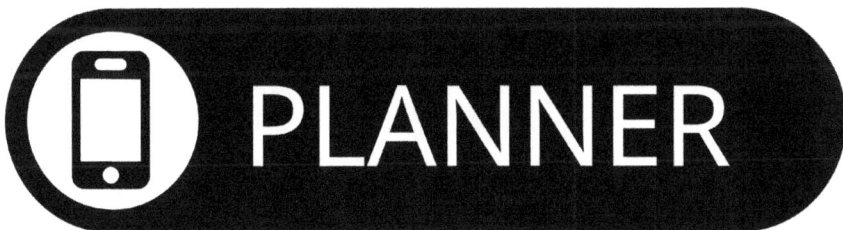

www.ingramcontent.com/pod-product-compliance
Lightning Source LLC
Chambersburg PA
CBHW060935220326
41597CB00020BA/3835